THE ART OF Tap Tuning

How to Build Great Sound into Instruments

by
Roger H. Siminoff

Edited by
Rosemary J Wagner

ISBN-13: 978-1-4234-2327-0

Copyright © 2006 by HAL LEONARD CORPORATION

All rights reserved. No part of this book may be reproduced in any form or by any electronic or mechanical means
including information storage and retrieval systems without permission in writing from the publisher,
except by a reviewer, who may quote brief passages in a review.

Published by:
Hal Leonard Corporation
7777 W. Bluemound Road
P.O. Box 13819
Milwaukee, WI 53213

In Australia Contact:
Hal Leonard Australia Pty. Ltd.
4 Lentara Court
Cheltenham, Victoria, 3192 Australia
Email: ausadmin@halleonard.com

Printed in the U.S.A.

First Edition

Visit Hal Leonard Online at
www.halleonard.com

Contents

Foreword iv
Preface v
Acknowledgments vii

Chapter 1, About Sound
Sound 1
Sound pressure 1
Compression and rarefaction 1
Transmission of sound 2
Frequencies and musical notes 3
Reflection and damping of sound 3
How string instruments generate sound 4
Vibrations of musical strings 4
Fundamentals 4
Partials 5
Attack 6
Lateral and longitudinal vibrations 6
Fixed and movable bridges 7
Energy transference via the bridge 7
String break angle 8
Loading the soundboard 8
Braces vs tone bars 9
The restoring force 9
Other factors that affect tuning:
  Bridge location 10
  Soundboard thickness 10
  Soundboard graduation 10
  Stiffness and pitch 10
  Other soundboard materials 11
  The ideal tap tuning reference note 11
  A variation on the premise of ideal reference .. 11

Chapter 2, Rationale for Tap Tuning
What is tap tuning? 12
Stiffness and frequency of wood parts 12
The body's contribution to tone 12
Tuning the air chamber 13
The body is an air pump 13
How sound is created 13
Communicating with the surrounding air 13
Parts tuned to a pitch 13
Determining the right note 14
Air chambers tuned to a pitch 15
Soundboard loading – the basic premise
  for tuning 15

Chapter 3, Factors That Affect the Tuning Process
Where to tap 17
Soundboard 17
Tone bars and braces 17
Backboard 18
Apertures 19

Chapter 3, cont'd
Air chamber 19
General tap tuning facts 19
Tone bar and brace location 21
Target tunings 22
The affects of finishes on tuning 23
Reference tuning 23

Chapter 4, Preparation for Tuning
The tuning process 24
Methods of tuning 24
Adjusting the air chamber 24
Tap hammers 25
Why strobe tuners for tap tuning? 25
Selecting a tuner 26
Setting up the tuner 26
Using a compressor 26
Interpreting the tapped tone 27
Reading the tuner 27
Changes you will discover 28
Test plates 28
Documenting your work 28

Chapter 5, Tuning and Voicing
Step 1 - Tune the soundboard 29
Step 2 - Tune the backboard 30
Step 3 - Tune the air chamber 30
Step 4 - Voice the air chamber 31
Repeatability 32

Chapter 6, Production Tuning
Deflection (structural) tuning 33
Example of deflection in adjustable bridge
  instruments 33
Example of deflection in fixed bridge
  instruments 33
Comparing deflection and tap tuning 34

Appendices
Appendix A, Tuning Record 35
Appendix B, Frequency Chart (*A*=440) 36
Appendix C, Target Tunings 37
Appendix D, A Brief History of Concert Pitch .. 38
Appendix E, *What Was Loar Hearing?* 40
Appendix F, More on Soundboards 43
Appendix G, Recommended Reading 46

References 46

Index 47

About the author 48

Foreword

Cliches come from some place. They are by nature, overused and increasingly diminished in value with each and every reference. They start out as an obvious expression of a common experience, and can often grow to be all-encompassing – such as "renaissance man" – which would have been coined to make it easy for me to present Roger Siminoff as an expert in many fields. Fortunately, I need to focus on only one: luthiery.

An anachronism before his time, this guy knows his stuff.

In *The Art of Tap Tuning,* Roger presents the definitive secret of the masters. While scientists have measured dimensions, calculated weights, and conducted chemical analysis of the works crafted by Stradivari, Amati, and the other luthiery illuminati, they have missed the point of what to quantify; it is the dang sound!

Roger Siminoff's credentials may lead one to expect some science speaking obsfucation. To the contrary, this text is born from numerous years of hands-on experience as Roger has shepherded many of the brightest brands and names in stringed instrument making into the golden age of luthiery. We, too, have felt his impact. Santa Cruz Guitars is now celebrating 30 years of guitar making, and I owe a great deal of our success to contributions he has made to the development of our guitars over the years. Now, in *The Art of Tap Tuning*, he gives us even more to think about.

Thanks, Roger, from all of us who follow in your wake.

Richard Hoover
President
Santa Cruz Guitar Company

Preface

When I hear an acoustic instrument, I hear a thousand voices. I've learned that the magic of the instrument's sound is far more than a single stream of musical elements. Instead, it is a rich integration of strings, harmonics, soundboard, backboard, air chamber, reflected sounds, and much more. All of these are present in the instrument's voice, and learning how to control and enhance the contribution of each part is a key component of the luthier's art.

Forty-five years ago when I started building acoustic instruments, it was fairly obvious to me that the job of the strings was to produce the sound, and the job of the air chamber was to amplify it. It all seemed quite simple! Yet, somehow, each of the instruments I built sounded different, even when I intensely focused on building each one precisely the same way and used the same type of strings. How could this be? What I thought was a simple scenario of the strings being the entire tone generator and the box being the amplifier turned out to be a complex interaction among all parts of the instrument in what acoustical engineers refer to as a "coupled system."

First, I learned that the strings were merely energy producers, and while the strings did impart a quality relative to their composition, structure, mass, and stiffness, their contribution to the instrument's overall tone was comparatively small. The soundboard, backboard, rim, air chamber, apertures, and even the neck were involved in contributing greatly to the overall tone.

Then I discovered that Mother Nature played a role in the process by creating wood that was so different board by board and inch by inch that I could not rely on physical measurements alone to provide similar tonal qualities in each instrument.

Lastly, it became obvious to me that all instruments had a unique identity: their components had a relationship to each other that provided a balance among the parts. For the instrument to be ideal, the strings had to be the right gauge and stiffness to fully impart their energy to the soundboard; the bridge at the right height and mass to efficiently transfer the strings' energy to the soundboard; the soundboard the right size and stiffness to be responsive to the strings' energy and to distribute that energy efficiently across its surface; the air chamber of a specific size that provided a resonant frequency to support the overall tonal range of the strings; the apertures of the correct size to efficiently tune the air chamber; the backboard tuned to a note that was harmonious to the air chamber's tuning; and the soundboard's bracings or tone bars tuned to notes equally harmonious to the air chamber's tuning that didn't cause "beats." Together, these parts are my "thousand voices" – a full orchestra of musical tones driven by the strings, but working together as a whole to provide the thick, rich voice of the instrument.

So, how do you achieve this balance and how do you replicate it?

That's what this book is about: the art of adjusting the tone of each part of a string musical instrument and being able to do it consistently. The book stresses the idea of "tap tuning," the art of adjusting the resonant frequency of a component to an ideal note or pitch. In the case of a soundboard or backboard and its affiliate bracing and/or tone bars, the adjustments are made to the stiffness (and mass). In the case of air chambers and apertures, the adjustments are made to their size. In all cases, the adjustments are based on the notes that are produced when the component or air chamber is excited (caused to vibrate). Since the process usually involves tapping on an object to excite it, the technique is referred to as "tap tuning."

Today, luthiers and historians often reflect on the work of the great violin makers of the Renaissance. We make extraordinary assumptions of the magical techniques these early builders employed from wizard wood-curing techniques to secret finish ingredients. On close examination, one thing rings clear as a tried and true technique – these great makers knew the value of component tuning and understood the contribution it made to their instruments' voices.

If we can successfully adjust the parts of the instrument to specific notes that are harmonious and are all full notes of the same scale (e.g., all part of the scale that is predicated on concert pitch

v

– A440 in 2007 – as its center point), then the instrument will be sonorous and provide a rich, brilliant voice.

By tuning each part individually, the entire instrument works as a whole with each part contributing its specific harmonious tonal quality to the overall sound of the instrument. And, we can carry this idea one step further by suggesting that each part of the instrument has unique attributes that can be modified to improve the overall performance of the instrument. For example, when an acoustic guitar is played, the resonant frequency of its air chamber can be heard along with the sound of the strings. Other components of the sound heard are the tones produced by the soundboard and backboard and the notes to which they are tuned. The strings provide the energy, but the entire sound we hear comes from all of the parts of the instrument acting as a whole. The sound dictated by the strings is now joined by the sound of the instrument's components. Change one part, and the entire instrument will sound differently.

The real mystique in tuning an instrument ends here – and it is here that the essence of building great sound into an instrument begins. This is the aspect of instrument construction, adjustment, and repair that requires you to listen and focus most intensely.

Many years ago while living in New Jersey, I had a baby grand piano that was of moderate make, vintage, and fair-to-poor tone, even when newly tuned. The aged soundboard was whole and was adorned with, if my memory serves me correctly, eleven brace bars. Lying under the piano one day, I banged on the bars and read the tone they produced using an early model Peterson strobe tuner. I discovered that only one brace bar was close to a note that was part of the A440 scale that the rest of the piano was tuned to. That discovery called out to me loud and clear. Beginning one Saturday, hand chisels and strobe tuner in hand, and lying flat on my back feeling very much like Michaelangelo painting the Sistine Chapel, I set out to tune the array of bars with the hope of breathing new life into this piano. It was a total labor of love, and about 60 hours of spare time later with wood chips scattered everywhere, I had a baby grand piano with tuned bars. I wish I had recorded the piano's sound before and after because the results were astonishing! I wouldn't say that the baby grand took on the voice of a Bosendorfer concert grand, but clearly it emerged as a new and important musical instrument in my home. And, all I did was tune part of its structure.

Although most of my focus over the past 45 years has been on tuning the bodies of banjos and mandolins, this text is not instrument specific. The concept of component tuning holds true whether you are building pianos, dulcimers, guitars, mandolins, banjos, violins, ukuleles, or any other acoustic string instrument.

While working with many folks over the phone who had trouble getting started with tap tuning and hearing the tapped tones, I was excited to learn that when I tapped on some tone bars – and they could fully concentrate on what they were hearing – they were able to easily identify the notes. It quickly became obvious that including some audio/video tracks with this text would help you hear and understand the attributes of tap tuning and give you a better appreciation for the process and results. To this end, I've prepared a DVD of several tests and demonstrations, and it is included at the back of this text.

I hope that gaining insight into the art of tap tuning will broaden your scope of building, add a new level of excitement to your craft, and improve the tonal quality of your instruments.

Happy tuning!
Roger H. Siminoff

Any description of products in this text does not constitute an endorsement by the author or by Hal Leonard Corporation, nor does it suggest that these are the best or only products of this type available at the time this text was written.

Author's contact information: web site: www.siminoff.net / email: siminoff@siminoff.net

Acknowledgments

My thanks to Richard Hoover of the Santa Cruz Guitar Company in Santa Cruz, CA for his kind opening words, to Joe Daoust of Lightening Joe's Guitar Heaven in Arroyo Grande, CA for allowing me to test his electronic gear, to Butch Boswell of Blue Note Guitars in San Luis Obispo, CA for letting me tap on their guitars for the acoustic tests, to Peter Morin for his excellent musicianship on the DVD, to Brad Smith of Hal Leonard Corporation for always believing in me, to Bruce Bolen and Jim Deurloo for letting me bring back tap tuning to Gibson in the '70s, to John Norris of PetersonElectro Musical for his frequencies and cents sense, to Brian Lawler for his video and graphics support, to Ron Saul for exploring the acoustics of his ukes and fiddles with me, to the countless luthiers who have shared their views with me on building and tuning, and to Rosemary Wagner who internalized, digested, reread, reorganized, consumed, and relentlessly edited this book.

To Zachary Aaron Siminoff
and
to my Rosemary, the source of my inspiration

and

to the memory of
Louise Scruggs
and
Charlie Derrington

THE ART OF Tap Tuning
How to Build Great Sound into Instruments

Periodic vibrations, whatever the source of sound, whatever the instrument used, always yield musical notes. They are smooth and agreeable to the ear, while, on the other hand, noises, or non-periodic vibrations, produce on the tympanic membrane a kind of jolting sensation. A sensation of irregularly recurring shocks.
<u>Sound and Music</u>, J. A. Zahm, A. C. McClurg & Co., Chicago, 1900

Chapter 1, About Sound

Sound:
At its most simple level, sound is the result of cause and effect.

Sound is produced when any object is set in motion and moves the air around it that, in turn, stimulates waves of air pressure to strike the eardrum (tympanic membrane). In this process, energy is transferred from the vibrating medium (the transmitter) to the eardrum (the receiver) resulting in a complex set of physiological activities that cause information to be sent to the brain. That information is what we perceive as sound.

If sound is dischordant, has irregular rhythm, and is generally unpleasant, we call it noise. If sound is pulsed in a way that it carries information we understand, we call it voice or signal. If it is chordant, rhythmic, and pleasant, we call it music.

We also qualify sound by how well or how poorly we receive it. If it comes to us with low energy, we say it is soft. If it comes to us with great energy, we say it is loud. Amplitude is the word we apply to describe an instrument's energy.

Timbre is the term we apply to musical sounds to describe their overall richness or color, sometimes called tone color. Lastly, clarity speaks about the ability to distinguish individual and beautifully shaped notes.

Amplitude, timbre, and clarity are qualities we seek to impart in our instruments. The instrument maker ("luthier" in the case of acoustic string instruments) acts somewhat paternal or maternal as he or she brings an instrument to life with these qualities, imparting to it a personality of its own.

Amplitude comes before sound, for it is the instrument's energy that drives the air masses so we can hear it. Of course, sound (like a singing voice) creates energy so some will argue which comes first, energy or sound. It's like arguing about the chicken or the egg. Suffice to say, energy and sound are very closely related.

Sound pressure:
Amplitude and loudness have some similarities and are often incorrectly used interchangeably, but each has a different meaning. Amplitude is a precise measurement by a device (typically a decibelometer) of the change in air pressure emitted from a sound-producing device. Amplitude is commonly based on a scale called decibels (dB) – a logarithmic formula in which each 3dB represents twice the sound pressure.

For most sounds, we typically don't feel the change in air pressure. But, you may have noticed that with very loud, shocking sounds (e.g., gunfire, backfire, fireworks, thunder, door slamming), you may actually feel the pressure as you hear the sound. Some everyday examples of dB values are: a whispered voice is about 35dB; normal office sounds (e.g., people speaking, office machines) measure approximately 50dB; an acoustic guitar played with a flatpick and measured three feet away generates about 80dB; and a twin engine jet aircraft taking off 200 yards away is approximately 130dB. Our threshold of pain for sound is about 130dB, and sound pressure above 130dB can cause physical damage to the delicate structure of the human ear. (Ear protection should always be worn when near any sound that exceeds 115dB.)

Loudness, on the other hand, is a human perception of how much sound is being emitted from a device depending on the surround or ambient noise. When you hear an alarm clock in the quiet of the morning, it appears very "loud." If the same alarm clock goes off when a large truck is going down the street outside of your bedroom, the clock doesn't seem as loud. And, if an alarm clock went off while you were standing near the runway of an airport as a jet was taking off, you probably wouldn't hear the alarm clock at all.

Compression and rarefaction:
As strings vibrate, they creates tiny waves of compression in the air they move toward and create tiny waves of rarefaction (the opposite of com-

pression) in the air they move away from. These tiny waves of compression and rarefaction from the strings are barely perceptible by themselves. However, if we attach the strings to a membrane – like the soundboard of a guitar or piano – larger waves of compression and rarefaction are generated. These larger waves have a positive effect on moving neighboring layers of air to and fro as the sound travels toward the receiving point (ear, microphone, etc.). Of course, we must balance the size of the strings (and the energy they can produce) with the size of the soundboard they are driving. Tiny strings are inadequate to drive the massive soundboard of a bass viol. Likewise, bass viol strings can exert too much energy for the tiny soundboard of a ukulele. If we are successful in matching the two elements, we can create a fairly effective air pump that transmits musical sounds.

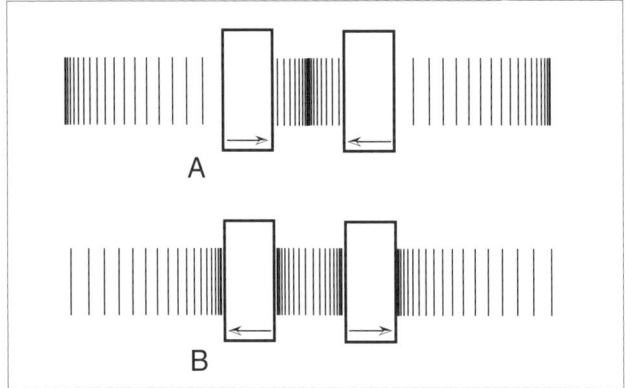

Fig. 1.1 When objects move toward each other, such as the blades of a tuning fork, (A) the layers of air between them are compressed (compression), and the air outside the blades is rarified (rarefaction). The process is reversed when the blades move apart (B).

Transmission of sound:
Sound can be transmitted through almost any medium (e.g., water, metal, wood, plastic, air). The denser and stiffer the medium, the more efficiently and clearly the sound is transmitted. As the material becomes less dense and approaches being porous, the sound is "damped" or absorbed and its efficiency and clarity are reduced. In this regard, sound starts as energy (vibrations) that travels through the medium. Assuming the vibrations are not damped (absorbed) and the vibrations are efficiently released into the air again, the vibrations move layers of air causing compression and rarefaction, the result of which is what we hear.

The damping of vibrations in wood is dependent on the wood's cellular structure, which varies by species. Spruce has a much higher anisotropic (transmission of energy) ratio than maple. Sound energy travels through spruce about ten times faster with the grain than across the grain. In maple, the ratio is only about four times faster with the grain than across the grain.

Sound can also be converted to electrical energy and transmitted through wires. Or, the electrical energy can be converted to ultra-high frequencies and transmitted through the air to be captured by antennas, amplified, and sent to speaker cones where it is converted back to changes in air pressure, and it again becomes the sound we hear. Thus, we have many ways to transmit sound (or more precisely, the energy representing sound), but only one way for us to hear the sound – our ears. Ultimately, sound is a form of energy.

Sound energy traveling through the air moves in pulses or layers of compression and rarefaction causing neighboring layers of air to move in compression and rarefaction. This movement of air is similar to ripples in a pool of water where each molecule of water doesn't actually move across the pool, but rather bumps the next molecule and retreats, resulting in only the last few molecules striking the shore. However, unlike ripples in water where the density doesn't change, the air becomes either more dense (compression) or less dense (rarefaction). Or, one might say it becomes compressed or rarefied.

When a tuning fork vibrates, the air on one side of a single fork blade is placed in compression while the air on the other side is in rarefaction. When the fork blade moves the other way, the compression and rarefaction are reversed and the air basically flows from one side of the blade to the other. The changing pressure, moving to and from the fork, is what we sense. As our tympanic membrane (in the ear) moves in concert with the movement of the air, it sets up a process in our inner ear that

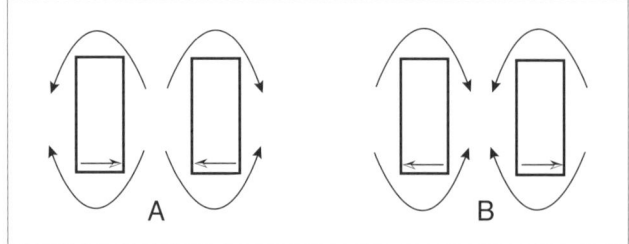

Fig. 1.2 Even though compression (A) and rarefaction (B) are occurring, the blades of the tuning fork are so small that the air can easily flow from one side of the blades to the other resulting in low amplitude.

Chapter 1, About Sound

transmits information to our brain and we "hear." Often, the blades of the tuning fork are too small to move a sufficient quantity of air for us to hear the sound. However, if we place the base of the

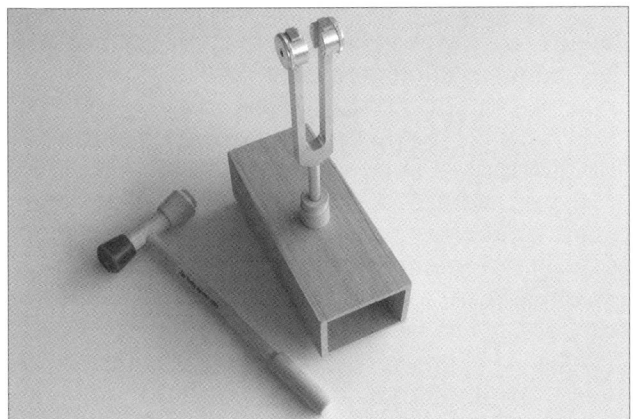

Fig. 1.3 Attaching the tuning fork to an air chamber improves the compression and rarefaction and greatly increases the amplitude of the tuning fork's energy.

fork against an object like a piece of wood (or better yet, an instrument's bridge or soundboard) the vibrations (or more specifically, the blades' energy) are transmitted to the soundboard. This enables larger masses of air to be moved, and we efficiently hear the sound from the tuning fork.

This, in essence, is how acoustic string instruments work: a small vibrating medium (the string) causes the soundboard to move, which in turn, causes compression and rarefaction inside the instrument's air chamber, which further causes compression and rarefaction to be directed out and away from the instrument until these waves of compression and rarefaction are recognized and recorded by the ear as sound.

Frequencies and musical notes:
The speed or rate at which the layers of air move is measured in pulses or vibrations per second. The vibrations or frequency are referred to as Hertz or Hz for short. (Years ago we used "cps" which stands for cycles-per-second.) For example, if there are 20 pulses of air per second, we say that the frequency is 20Hz. If the pulses are an even rate (e.g., a constant 20Hz for a period of time), we hear a tone. If the pulses are erratic (e.g., first 20Hz, then 5000Hz, then 600Hz, and so on in rapid, quickly changing pulses), we hear noise. If the frequencies change at a particular cadence, have a pleasant relationship to one another, and are not so loud that they are overbearing, what we hear is music (we hope). Thus, the major

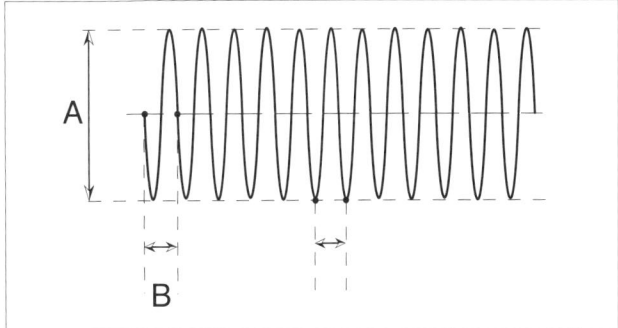

Fig. 1.4 Amplitude (A) is a measurement of the strength of the signal (perceived as loudness). Frequency (B) is a measurement of the number of complete cycles of energy per second, which can also be measured (but less correctly) from pulse to pulse (C).

difference between noise, tone, and music, is the order, cadence, and intensity of the pulses.

Objects that vibrate at a controlled rate produce a tone or note. A tuning fork is an example of an object whose length and stiffness are adjusted so that it vibrates at a specific rate. A tuning fork that vibrates 440 times per second (440Hz) produces the musical note A, and a tuning fork that vibrates 261.63 times per second (261Hz) produces the musical note C.

Depending on the listener's age and physical condition, a person can hear a frequency range from approximately 15Hz to about 18,000Hz. Younger people (age 20 and below) have a slightly greater upper threshold and can typically hear up to about 20,000Hz. At about 12Hz and below, the continuous tone becomes a series of distinct beats or pulses. The lowest note on a piano is 1st octave C at 32.70Hz, but one could create notes as low as sub-1st octave D at 18.36Hz, and it could still be perceived as a very low, continuous tone.

Reflection and damping of sound:
Sound energy can be reflected away from any surface. The smoother the surface, the better the reflection. As the surface becomes less smooth, the waves of sound get diffused, are spread over a larger area, and the sound pressure reflected in any one specific direction is reduced. If the surface is smooth and convex, the sound will be diffused to several points. If the surface is smooth and concave, the sound can be focused to a specific distant point. Ideally, the inside surfaces of an instrument's air chamber should be smooth. They need not be painted or polished, but a smooth finish is important to reduce diffusion and damping.

The Art of Tap Tuning

Sound energy can be absorbed or damped by a surface that is soft, porous, or baffle-shaped. The thicker the material, the greater the damping qualities because sound waves can penetrate deeply and do not rebound. Avoiding a surface that features all three (soft, porous, and baffle-shaped) is important.

Sound energy can also be damped when it travels through a non-resilient material. Some examples of this are: the tin-can-and-string walkie-talkies when the string is slack or a plastic bell compared to a brass bell. Typically, the less dense the material, the greater its absorption properties. Conversely, the denser the material, the greater its transmissive properties. A major characteristic of the various species of wood is the great difference of their densities and mass. In this regard, it is important to appreciate the attributes of various species of wood and their contributions to sound and tone production when building wood bodied musical instruments. (For more information on the tonal contribution of various species of woods, see *The Luthier's Handbook*, Hal Leonard Corporation, Milwaukee, WI.)

As stated previously, sound energy can be amplified as when the small vibrations of musical strings are enhanced by being connected to a soundboard. Of course, electronic methods can be used to capture vibrations, convert them to electrical energy, amplify the energy, and play it back through a sound-pressure producing device like the paper cone in a conventional speaker. Herein lies the major difference in the requirements of an acoustic string instrument with its carefully tuned air chamber and an electric instrument (typically with no air chamber) and its electric pickups that sense the strings' vibrations and convert them to electrical energy.

Sound energy can be modified. On electric instruments, we have sophisticated technology to adjust amplitude, trim treble, mid-tones, and bass, and to add a plethora of effects to make nearly any tone imaginable. With non-electric acoustic string musical instruments, we adjust the tonal characteristics of the instrument by how we work the wood and how we tune the various components of the instrument.

We can adjust the tone and amplitude of an acoustic string instrument by making adjustments to string tension, bridge height, bridge position, soundboard thickness, soundboard graduation rate (how and where it gets thick and thin), soundboard bracing and tone bars (stiffness, size, and location), soundpost location (viol family), apertures (oval, round, or *f*-hole size and location), tailpiece length and stiffness, size of air chamber, shape of air chamber, and instrument's finish.

How string instruments generate sound:
On all acoustic string instruments, the strings are the energizers (actually the fingers, picks, hammers, or bows provide the initial energy). The energy from the strings causes the bridge to move which, in turn, excites the soundboard. When the soundboard vibrates, it moves masses of air in front of and behind it, causing layers of compression and rarefaction to emanate from the instrument. When we place a carefully constructed air chamber behind the soundboard and perforate the soundboard's surface with carefully sized and tuned apertures (i.e., *f*-holes, oval soundhole, or round soundhole), we not only amplify the strings' energy, but we add "voicing" to it and can control the richness and "color" (timbre) of the sound.

<u>The overall tone of the instrument – that is, the timbre it produces – comes from the components of the instrument and not from the strings.</u> The strings produce the energy; the body produces the tone. You will learn in this text that it is the careful balance of the gauge and tension of the strings, the size and height of the bridge, the size and stiffness (tuning) of the soundboard, and most importantly, the tuning of the air chamber and its apertures that work together as a whole to give the instrument a rich and powerful tone.

Vibrations of musical strings:
Musical strings vibrate in different modes or sections, sometimes vibrating as a whole length of the string, other times vibrating in two segments (one half of the string moving one way while the other half moves the opposite way), or in thirds, in fourths, and so on. In addition to vibrating and creating energy by moving side to side as one can easily imagine, strings also transmit energy lengthwise. These lengthwise or longitudinal vibrations are as important in some instruments as the side to side (lateral) vibrations are to other instruments.

Fundamentals:
When a string vibrates as a whole (Fig. 1.5) the note it produces is called the fundamental. For

Chapter 1, About Sound

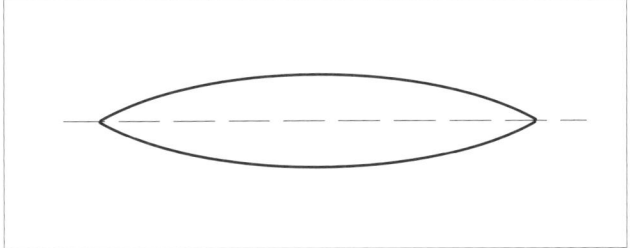

Fig. 1.5 The fundamental, also referred to as the "first partial" is produced when a string vibrates in one whole segment. This is the lowest note a string can produce at a specific tension.

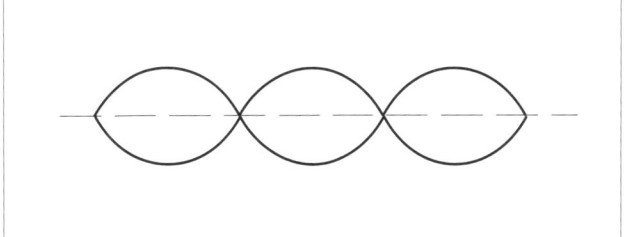

Fig. 1.7 The third partial occurs when the string vibrates in thirds. The string also vibrates in fourths, fifths, sixths, and so on.

example, if a string is tuned to 440Hz (*A*440 or the fourth octave *A*), the *A* note it produces when it vibrates as a whole is called the fundamental. The fundamental is the lowest note the string can produce and is the basic note to which the string is tuned (without being fretted). More specifically, the fundamental is the note the string produces when it vibrates in one whole movement – the entire length of string moving to one side or the other. The *A*440 string can produce higher tones or partials, but it cannot produce any note lower than *A*440 while at its specific tension.

Partials:
The same *A* string can also begin to vibrate in two equal segments or halves producing vibrations that are twice as fast as the fundamental (Fig. 1.6). Since the *A* is 440Hz, the sound produced by the string vibrating in two halves (which produces vibrations that are twice as fast) is 880Hz (440+440=880), a note that is one octave above *A*440; *A*880 – the fifth octave *A*.

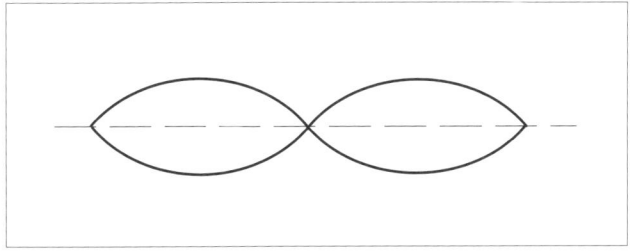

Fig. 1.6 The second partial is produced when a string vibrates in two segments. Because these vibrations are twice as fast as the fundamental, they produce a note that is an octave above the fundamental.

Further, the string also vibrates in thirds (Fig. 1.7), and produces a note that is a fifth above the *A*880. This note is at the frequency of 1320Hz (440+440+440=1320) which is the sixth octave *E* or *E*1320. It then vibrates in fourths (440+440+440+440=1760) which is the next octave *A* or *A*1760, and so on.

How does it do this? It is a natural phenomenon that primarily depends on: a) where the string is played [*location of attack* – i.e., near the end of the string vs in the middle]; b) how hard the string is played [*method of attack* – i.e., plucked, hammered, or bowed]; c) how long it is played [*duration of attack* – i.e., continuous bowing or singular picking]; and d) the nature and strength of restoring forces. All things that vibrate move in various complex modes.

These parts of the whole motion of the string are called partials, and the string's overall tone is comprised of as many as 16 to 18 different audible partials. Therefore, the overall tone or timbre of a string is comprised of many discrete tones called the harmonic series. How much overall tone the human ear can detect is determined by the amplitude (loudness) and frequency of each of the partials. And, of course, for the higher partials to be heard, they must be within the range of human hearing.

The partials are numbered from one (1st) to as many as can be detected (heard). The 1st partial is the fundamental or entire singular vibration of the string. Again, this is the lowest note that a string can produce while at a specific tension and without being fretted. So, in the case of the previous example of the *A*440 string, the 440Hz *A* note is both the 1st partial and the fundamental. The 2nd partial is when the string vibrates in halves, the 3rd partial is when it vibrates in thirds, and so on. The combination of partials and their relative amplitudes (loudness) give the string its timbre or color, that is then transferred to the soundboard. Typically, even-numbered partials (2nd, 4th, 6th, and so on) produce warmer tones than odd-numbered partials (1st, 3rd, 5th, and so on). Thus, when a string is played or picked such that its odd-numbered partials have greater amplitude than its even-numbered partials, it will sound brighter than a string that produces greater amplitude on

The Art of Tap Tuning

its even-numbered partials. The corollary is when a string is played such that its even-numbered partials have greater amplitude than its odd-numbered partials, it will sound warmer or mellower.

On non-keyboard acoustic string instruments, the musician playing has control over the partials based on the method of attack and location of attack. This can be easily heard by comparing an instrument being played near the bridge (brighter sound) to it being played further away from the bridge (warmer sound). The musician is merely exciting different sets of partials.

We can hear individual partials, which are called "harmonics" when they are isolated. A harmonic is created by forcing a node or null point in the string, which causes the string to vibrate primarily in one of its partial modes. For example, a harmonic can be produced by placing the finger lightly on the string at a point that is one-half the string's length (above the 12th fret on a fretted instrument). This forces the string to vibrate in halves to produce the 2nd partial. Coincidentally, this mode of vibration produces a note that is an octave above the fundamental. Thus, a string that vibrates at 440Hz (4th octave A) will produce a note that is 5th octave A at 880Hz when it is forced into a harmonic at its 12th fret or mid-point position.

So, partials and harmonics are related, but different. A harmonic is the *sound* produced by forcing a string to vibrate in segments; partials are the *numerical order* of the various frequencies – including the fundamental – that a string can produce.

Attack:
The acoustic string instrument families sound different from each other because the various combinations of the method, duration, and location of attack excite different partials on different instruments. For method and duration, consider picked vs bowed, hammered vs strummed, and plastic flatpicks vs metal fingerpicks. And, for location, consider near the bridge, away from the bridge, and near the neck heel. All of these combinations produce very different sounds from the identical string and instrument.

A good example of the relevance and impact of the location of attack is found in the design of better pianos. Looking inside a quality grand piano, you will notice that each of the hammers is positioned at a point that is 1/7 of the string's length (actually, you see the dampers – the hammers are immediately below the dampers). You see that the row of dampers is at an angle from the piano's bridge so that the longest string is attacked at a point 1/7 of its length as is the shortest string. This assures that the location of attack causes the same series of partials to be excited on all strings in the piano in an effort to have all strings deliver similar timbre.

As with strings, soundboards vibrate in modes. The position of the bridge on the soundboard, as well as the location of the tone bars and braces, is as important to the timbre of the instrument as is where the strings are picked.

Lateral and longitudinal vibrations:
As stated previously, musical strings produce energy both laterally and longitudinally. These modes have different levels of importance based on whether the instrument is designed with a fixed or movable bridge.

Lateral vibrations are those motions that go in a complex orbit of up and down and side to side, parallel to the length of the string; longitudinal vibrations travel directly through the length of the string from the nut to the bridge (Fig. 1.8). Further, there are two forms of longitudinal vibrations: a) those that travel directly through the center axis of the string – through the wire itself as a result of its elasticity and changes in tension; and b) those that are basically longitudinal but snap along the length of the string, driving energy to one end or the other. The two forms of longitudinal vibrations are far stronger than the lateral ones at any one point along the string's length. While the energy from lateral vibrations is distributed along the

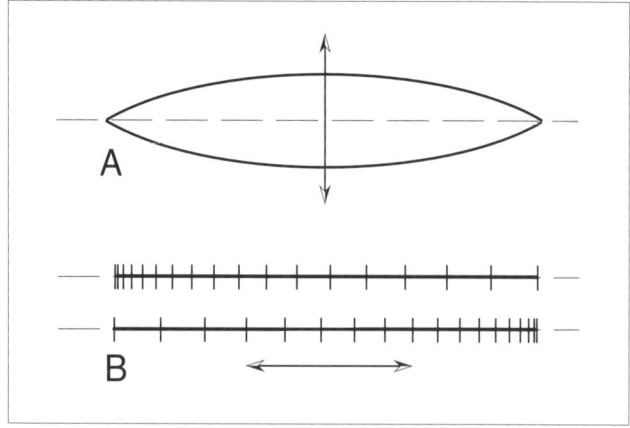

Fig. 1.8 A string produces energy in two directions: lateral (A) and longitudinal (B). The design of the instrument (i.e., fixed bridge vs movable bridge) can take advantage of either or both of these modes.

Chapter 1, About Sound

string's length, the greatest amplitude is typically in the center of the string. By comparison, all of the energy from longitudinal vibrations is sent to each end of the string.

Let's consider the soundboard of an acoustic guitar with a fixed bridge and no tailpiece. This soundboard is driven almost entirely by longitudinal vibrations pulling at (and releasing) the bridge, resulting in the bridge and soundboard being torqued or twisted back and forth on the bridge's centerline axis. This motion forces the soundboard to act as the bellows of an air pump causing compression and rarefaction inside the guitar's soundbox. This same air pump action occurs on members of the viol family. However, in the viol family, the lateral vibrations are of greater importance than the longitudinal ones because of the high string angle over the bridge, the way the soundboard is loaded by the strings' pressure on the bridge, the location of a single soundpost, the strings' anchoring at the tailpiece, and the continuous side-to-side motion of the bow.

In considering longitudinal vibrations, when a string is brought to pitch, there is equal tension at both the tuning peg and the tailpiece. Musical strings are flexible and can stretch similar to an elastic cord. For example, a .010″ plain E string (on a 13.5″ string scale) exerts about 13 pounds of tension (e.g., the pegbox and tailpiece are being pulled towards each other with 13 pounds of force). In this example, the .010″ plain E string stretches slightly more than 1/16″ (1.6mm) when brought up to pitch. The string can stretch a little bit more but it will also reach a point where it can stretch no more, loses tone color, and is at a point where it can rupture.

When plucked or bowed, the string stretches and the tension between the pegbox and tailpiece increases; then as the sidewards motion slackens, the tension decreases. The energy driven toward both ends of the string actually reduces the string's tension for a fraction of a second, and it does this repeatedly. So, for that fraction of a second, after a single E string is played on a mandolin with normal picking energy, it could increase the string's tension by 1 to 2 pounds, with the total tension increasing to 14 or 15 pounds. When the string slackens, some of this slackening process drives the energy to the ends of the string (longitudinally) resulting in a reduction of the string's tension – for just a fraction of a second – to 12.5 or 12 pounds. So, the nut and bridge in this example are actually receiving longitudinal shock loads ranging from 12 to 15 pounds!

Fixed and movable bridges:
Knowledge of lateral and longitudinal vibrations helps to understand and envision how fixed and movable bridge systems function differently. Theoretically, the fixed bridge system utilizes a higher percentage of the strings' energy than instruments with tailpieces because a tailpiece captures the tension and absorbs some of the strings' energy.

On fixed bridge instruments, the coupled bridge/soundboard combination is driven by energy from the strings' longitudinal vibrations. In reality, the bridge on a fixed bridge system utilizes about 60% of the energy because the other 40% is absorbed by the neck, nut, and tuning machines. What is actually used by the instrument to produce tone and what is absorbed or damped by the instrument itself is another matter. This is a very good reason to build stiff, solid necks that are well fitted to the instrument's body, with dense bone or similar nuts, and a rigid truss rod system. The less energy the neck can absorb, the more there is to drive the bridge.

In movable bridge systems (mandolins, banjos, viol-family instruments) where the strings' tension is captured by a tailpiece, the lateral vibrations become the important energy producers. The bridge and soundboard function in an entirely different manner than on fixed bridge instruments. The soundboard is placed under load and responds to the lateral slackening and tensioning of the strings. (While some sound is produced as a result of the string being connected to the peghead – and butt of the instrument on movable bridge instruments – the contribution to the overall sound of the instrument is minimal.)

Energy transference via the bridge:
On fixed bridge steel string and classical guitars, the energy is transferred to the bridge causing it to rock back and forth on its axis and flex the soundboard. On movable bridge instruments, the energy is transferred to the soundboard through an up and down motion of the bridge. In this case, some of the longitudinal vibrations to the tailpiece do transfer minimal energy to the soundboard through the tailblock as well as from the nut, down through the neck to the headblock. However, on the mandolin and viol-family instruments, the soundboard loading and energy production come mainly through the bridge. On these instruments,

The Art of Tap Tuning

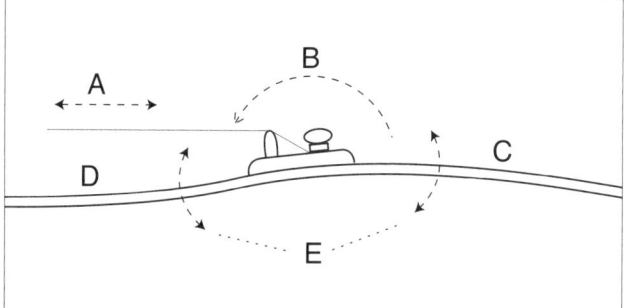

Fig. 1.9 On a fixed bridge instrument, the longitudinal vibrations (A) of the string play a critical role by driving the bridge through a rocking motion. The soundboard is torqued at the bridge (B) causing a bulge behind the bridge (C) and a hollow in front of the bridge (D). This leads to a pumping action (E).

the amount of energy the strings can transmit to the bridge is dependent on the angle at which the strings cross over the bridge. This determines how much pressure forces the bridge down to the soundboard. The viol-family instruments employ a post under the treble foot of the bridge to increase the stiffness of the soundboard, drive some energy to the backboard, while all the time directing most of the energy to the bass bar.

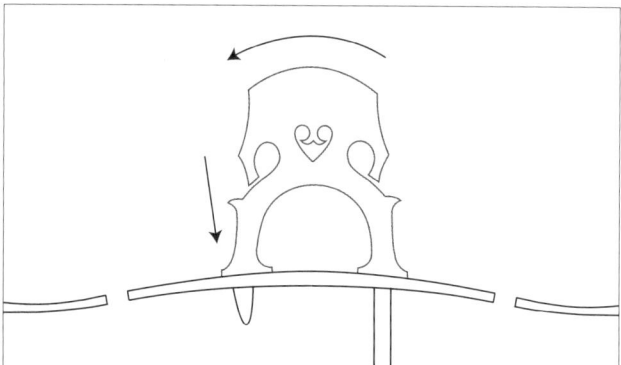

Fig. 1.10 The soundpost in the viol-family instruments plays several roles: it couples the soundboard and backboard; it raises the resonant frequency of the air chamber – a result of stiffening the soundboard and backboard; it damps unwanted overtones; and it provides a fulcrum for the bridge to rock upon and drive energy to the soundboard via the bass bar.

String break angle:
On movable bridge instruments, the angle the strings make over the bridge is called the "string break angle." Envision for a moment if the strings went straight back to the tailpiece and just touched the bridge; you would hear very little aside from string buzzes. The greater the angle, the more the strings' energy is driven toward the soundboard. There are limits, though, because too much

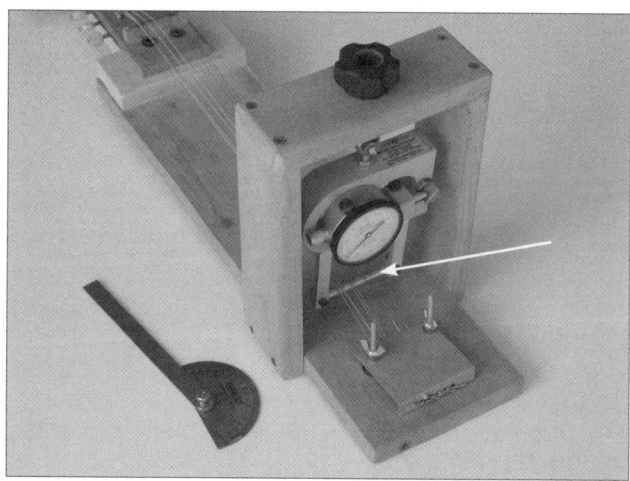

Fig. 1.11 This fixture measures the down pressure of the strings at the bridge. A surrogate bridge (arrow) is attached under the Dillon® Certified Force Gauge and can be raised or lowered until the desired string break angle is achieved. The test in this photo determined that a set of D'Addario® J60 mandolin strings presented a downward load of 38 pounds at a 16° string break angle (angle of strings over the bridge).

pressure can cause the bridge to rupture or the soundboard to implode.

Some musicians assert that bridge height is the most important thing in sound production. Considering bridge height by itself is meaningless. From a playing standpoint, bridge height is only relative to achieving good playing action in the upper fret positions. So, you might consider that bridge height and neck angle go hand in hand. Bridge height is a factor of proper neck angle or neck pitch. Bridge height and neck angle taken together, and the location where the strings connect to the tailpiece, contribute to the string break angle over the bridge. The greater the neck angle, the taller the bridge – but the string break angle also increases. The lower the next angle, the lower the bridge – and the string break angle then also decreases. The string break angle, not the bridge height itself, determines how much load is driven down to the soundboard.

Loading the soundboard:
The soundboard gets "loaded" when the strings are brought up to tension. For example, on an F-style mandolin with medium gauge strings and a 16° string break angle over the bridge there is about 38 pounds of down pressure on the soundboard. The load or pressure of the strings pushes down on the soundboard via the bridge and places the soundboard in a state of compression. How-

Chapter 1, About Sound

ever, the soundboard, under the strings' compression, pushes back with a force equal to the strings (about 38 pounds) and a stasis or neutral point is reached. If stasis didn't occur, the strings would keep pushing down until the soundboard flattened or imploded, or the soundboard would keep pushing up until the strings' pitch changed or the strings burst. Thus, we say the soundboard is "loaded" and prepared to be responsive to any vibration coming its way via the strings. When the strings tighten, the soundboard moves down; when the strings slacken the soundboard moves up. Of course, this happens hundreds of times per second in a wide array of frequencies and amplitude ranges. The soundboard also moves in numerous modes of its own, but those driven by the strings are the basic movements that produce the majority of the energy that emanates from the instrument.

Braces vs tone bars:
On a flat-top acoustic guitar, internal bracing is important to keep the large, flat soundboard from bending out of shape or self-destructing as well as to control the amount of stiffness of the soundboard. By comparison, on a mandolin or violin, the arched and graduated soundboard is a very strong and deflection-resistant shape so braces are not needed for strength. Instead, tone bars are used to adjust the stiffness of the soundboard and are an important element of the tuning process. Basically, braces and tone bars are both pieces of wood glued to the underside of a soundboard. The only difference between them is how they are used and the job they perform: a brace is for structure and a tone bar is for tuning.

The restoring force:
A restoring force is stored energy that reinforces a string's vibrations after it is attacked. The restoring force is the result of the string's energy being transferred to another element of the instrument – the soundboard, for example – and then transferred back to the string.

Aside from bowed instruments, the primary restoring force on string instruments is the energy inherent in the tension of strings that are tuned to pitch. The secondary restoring force comes from the components of the instrument. However, on most string instruments, the soundboard and backboard damp and/or use as much energy as they restore. If you were to stretch a musical string between two concrete walls so that nothing could damp its vibrations and then tune the string up to pitch and attack it, the vibrations would continue for a slightly extended period of time – more so than the same string would on a musical instrument. This is due to the tension and resilience of the string acting as stored energy that is not being damped by some connected element. Thus, as the string is played, the string tightens and increases the tension; as the string slackens, the tension in various portions of the string is lessened (and so on) as the string continues to vibrate.

Simply stated, a restoring force is transferred energy initially stimulated by the string that helps the string sustain. While the soundboard can have a damping affect, the energy from the loaded soundboard can help restore the string's vibrations and, in this case, the soundboard would be a restoring force. The stiffness and resilience of the neck provides an additional restoring force but, as previously mentioned, about 40% of the string's energy is absorbed by the neck.

The restoring force is a key element in producing sustain. Sustain is the quality we attribute to a string or an instrument that continues to generate energy long after the string is attacked. On a violin, the main force that keeps the string in motion is the energy that comes from the bow's continuous movement. In this case, the instrument's body plays a comparatively small role in providing a restoring force.

However, on the violin, the restoring force can also be the instrument's worst enemy. Let's assume for a moment that we have a violin with an air chamber that is tuned to a D♭. The violinist bows a D♭ note and drives the string with some assertion so that it sustains for a brief period. At first, the air chamber reacts wildly because its resonant frequency – the D♭ – has been excited. Then the air chamber responds, in the form of a restoring force and drives energy back to the string. The string, stimulated by the restoring force and still being bowed, now produces energy with greater intensity than before, and sends energy back to the air chamber which, in turn, sends energy back to the string. If this bowing and air chamber exchange continues, an unwanted howling effect will begin to occur. This unpleasant "woo woo woo woo" sound is referred to as a "wolf note" or "wolf tone." Once the bowing stops, the energy of the restoring force is eliminated and the howling ends.

We don't typically hear wolf notes on non-bowed acoustic instruments because the singular picked

The Art of Tap Tuning

attack and quickly following decay are almost instantaneous rather than the long sustain of the constantly bowed violin.

One last point on restoring force: The string's lateral energy causes the string to vibrate in an orbit around the string's axis. Looking down the length of a string while it is vibrating, you would see that the lateral vibrations move in a circular direction around the string's center axis. In addition, you might also notice that more vibrations appear to occur up and down (Fig. 1.12) – to and from the soundboard – than sideways, the direction in which they began. This is due to the restoring force; the energy that is sent back to the string via the bridge tends to be in an up-and-down motion and causes the string to vibrate in that orbit. This is an interesting phenomenon when considering that the string is first set into motion sideways (that is, first picked in a side-to-side motion). Some of the lateral motion (orbits) results from imperfect hexagonal-core wire on the wound strings, but that is beyond the scope of this text.

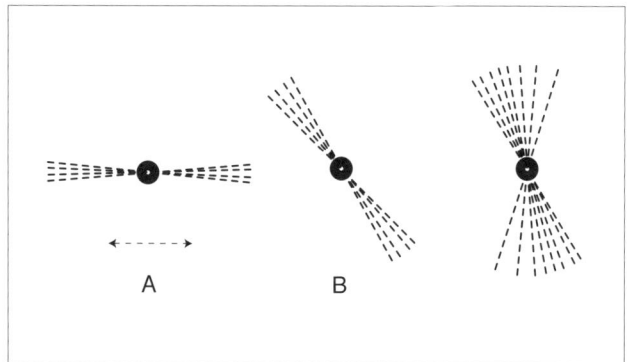

Fig. 1.12 When a string is first played (A), the lateral vibrations begin in a plane that responds to the attack of the pick (arrow). Typically, this is somewhat parallel to the soundboard. After a few seconds, if not played again, the string begins to orient into a mode that is more perpendicular to the soundboard (B & C).

Other factors that affect tuning:

Bridge location:
The location of the bridge on the soundboard is as important as the location of attack on the string. Each soundboard has vibrational modes of its own and these modes also include partials. The exact point where the soundboard is excited or driven is very important to both the amplitude and the tonal properties of the instrument. The closer the bridge is to the edge of the soundboard, as in the case of the bridge location on a piano soundboard, the brighter, snappier but more muted the sound becomes. The closer the bridge is toward the center of the soundboard, the more mellow, warm, and full the sound becomes. The exact location of the bridge is a result of the instrument's design and depends on the string scale (distance from nut to bridge) and fretboard location.

Soundboard thickness:
To be effective as a tone producer, the soundboard must be supple. If it is too stiff, it will be incapable of flexing and will be unable to cause compressive force within the air chamber. If it is too limber, it will damp vibrations and the energy of the strings will quickly decay. Most soundboard woods (spruce, cedar, etc.) become reasonably flexible when prepared to about .110″ (2.8mm) to .115″ (2.9mm) thick.

Soundboard graduation:
For the sake of amplitude and clarity, the soundboard has to work primarily as one whole unit and not as numerous smaller vibrational areas. If the soundboard were to pulse in numerous regions and modes, the compressive force of one area would tend to cancel or null the rarefactive force of another area. To accomplish the aspect of wholeness and to direct the strings' energy from the bridge across the entire soundboard in singular massive movements, the soundboard should be built structurally from the center outwards. In this regard, a flat soundboard, whose entire surface is the same thickness as in the case of an acoustic guitar, would have its concentration of braces and tone bars in the center with each element tapering to thinness just before it reaches the rim (rib) where it gets thicker again for attachment. Or, in the case of the viol-family and movable bridge instruments with graduated soundboards and backboards, the carving of the soundboard should be prepared so that the soundboard is thicker in the center than it is near its edges.

Stiffness and pitch:
Stiffness and pitch are inextricably connected. For example, if you precisely tune a guitar's plain E string and then measure its exact tension, you might get something like 13.655 pounds. If you then slacken that string and bring it back to exactly 13.655 pounds, it will again be tuned to precisely an E. And, as you know, if you increase the tension, the pitch of the string rises; if you reduce the tension, the pitch of the string drops. This is the same phenomenon that happens when tuning wood parts of an instrument. If you reduce the stiffness of a tone bar or brace, you will lower its resonant frequency (the note it makes when it

Chapter 1, About Sound

is tapped). Similarly, the stiffer a soundboard or backboard, the higher the note will be; and the more supple (thinner) a soundboard or backboard, the lower the note.

Other soundboard materials:
The soundboards (heads) on banjos are made of either skin or Mylar®, and the mechanical attributes of these instruments make them very tunable by simply tightening or loosening the head. Banjo apertures are adjusted by re-positioning the height of the pot assembly into the resonator. While there is no specific reference to the tap tuning process for banjos in this text, I do provide tuning references in Appendix C. (For more information on tuning techniques for banjos, see *How to Set Up the Best Sounding Banjo*, Hal Leonard Corporation, Milwaukee, WI.)

The ideal tap tuning reference note:
With the knowledge that the various parts of the instrument produce a note when excited, we are plagued with finding a satisfactory note in which to tune the cavity and parts of an instrument. As you will see in Chapter 5 that covers tuning the air chamber, to prevent the symptom of wolf notes, we need to find notes for the body parts that are part of the *A440* scale. However, in using a note that is part of our concert-tuned scale, the instrument will be "hot" when that particular note is played, and a component of the body tuned to that note is excited. Take, for example, a guitar whose soundboard, backboard, and air chamber are all tuned to a *G*. What do you think happens when a *G* note or *G* chord is played? Yes, the instrument shouts! Musicians typically want their acoustical instruments to be powerful – but not just on one note!

So, one important lesson is that we want components of the instrument (soundboard, backboard, air chamber) to be tuned to notes that are part of the *A440* scale but won't create wolf notes. On the other hand, we want the parts to be tuned to notes less typically played so that the instrument doesn't shout when a single note or relative chord is played. This is what *The Art of Tap Tuning* is all about, and you will learn how to accomplish this task later on in this text.

A variation on the premise of ideal reference:
There is another approach to concert-pitch tuning that yields exceptional-sounding instruments, but the method requires a brief introduction.

Among the most heralded of tuned acoustic string instruments are the Master Model guitars, mandolas, and mandolins produced by Gibson Inc. in the period of 1920 to 1925 (then known as The Gibson Mandolin-Guitar Manufacturing Company). These instruments boasted a label that stipulated that the soundboard, backboard, and air chamber of the instrument were tuned and approved by Gibson's acoustical engineer, Lloyd A. Loar (1886-1943).

In February, 2006, there was a "LoarFest West" event in Bakersfield, California where about two dozen Loar-signed Gibson F5 mandolins were on display for musicians, luthiers, and fans to inspect and hear. While each instrument had its own character, the instruments played in that room shared an incredible tonal resemblance unlike any two, three, or four mandolins I have ever heard in the same place at the same time. Clearly, it was a testament to the virtues and credibility of tap tuning.

What is especially unusual about the incredible voice of these instruments today is their tuning. In 1920, Loar and most of the music world did not use *A440* as concert pitch, but instead tuned to notes that used *C256* as reference (*C256* resides on a scale that has *A* at 431Hz). The quarter-tone difference delivers exceptional timbre to the instrument and provides a valuable lesson. For more information on the background of Loar's tuning process and what makes these instruments sound the way they do today, see Appendix E, *What Was Loar Hearing?* And, for more information on how concert pitch has changed through the years, see Appendix D, *A Brief History of Concert Pitch*.

Further reading:
For more on soundboards and how they work, an interesting article written by Lloyd Loar in 1925 entitled "*What Soundboards Do And How They Do It*" is included in Appendix F.

Small changes in the height of the bass bar can shift not only the frequency of the tap tone, but also the shape of the tap tone resonance.
Physics and the Sound of Music, John S. Rigden, John Wiley and Sons, New York, 1977

Chapter 2, Rationale for Tap Tuning

What is tap tuning?
Tap tuning is the process of adjusting the stiffness of individual parts of an instrument to control how each contributes to the overall tone or timbre of the instrument. To measure stiffness, the part is set into motion (by tapping or bowing) to determine the note or frequency it produces. Adjustments are then made to the stiffness of the part until the desired tuning note is reached. As a result, the tuning provides a measurement of how stiff the part is (tuning and stiffness are related), and this leads to building excellent sounding instruments that are consistent.

In practice, tap tuning is used to assess and adjust the stiffness of a soundboard or backboard, and to determine and adjust the size of the aperture(s) that lead to the air chamber of an acoustic string instrument so that the instrument's body is sonorous, projects well, promotes a rich sound, is absent of unwanted "beats" or dischordant tones, and most importantly, responds evenly and equally to all notes.

Contrary to popular opinion, "tap tuning" is not magic that can only be performed by someone with incredible skills. Tap tuning is a comparatively simple art that is not much more complicated than tuning the pairs of strings on a mandolin or a 12-string guitar. In fact, the idea of tuning the structural parts of an instrument is very similar to the idea of tuning the strings. The core premise is that the structural parts play as important a role, if not more important, in the overall sound of the instrument than the strings do. This overall sound is the result of the separate parts acting as a whole in what acoustical engineers call a coupled system. It is, therefore, important to control how the structural parts produce tone. Through the tap tuning process, all parts of the instrument are brought into a harmonious balance so they contribute to the tone of the instrument, making the entire instrument work as a whole.

Tap tuning is also a method of confirming that the parts of the instrument are prepared to the correct stiffness as well as to the correct size. It ensures that each piece of wood prepared will react in a similar way. The determination of soundboard and backboard thickness, size of the soundhole(s), and the actual size of the air chamber are all factors that are established and verified by the tuning process. With the aid of a frequency measuring device, the process of finding the pitch of each part is greatly simplified. These adjustments result in a properly tuned instrument with a rich voice that comes alive in the musician's hands.

Stiffness and frequency of wood parts:
In the same way that the stiffness and pitch of musical strings are related (*Stiffness and pitch*, page 10), the stiffness and frequency (pitch) of wood parts are related. As the stiffness of a given piece of wood is decreased, its pitch is decreased. And, if we increase the stiffness of a piece of wood by adding braces or tone bars, its pitch would increase. In essence, we know something about the stiffness of a piece of wood if we can determine the pitch to which it is tuned. *The stiffness of a piece of wood has a direct relationship to its resonant frequency. Conversely, the resonant frequency of a piece of wood has a direct relationship to its stiffness.*

The body's contribution to tone:
It is important to remember that on an acoustic string instrument, the strings do not produce the timbre of the sound. They provide the *frequency* and the *energy* that produces the sound. When a string or combination of strings is played, it excites the instrument's structure by driving energy through the bridge to the soundboard, which in turn excites the air in the body of the instrument, sets the backboard in motion, and begins the process of creating waves of air movement (compression and rarefaction) that ultimately become the sound we hear. *The strings determine the frequency and provide the energy to cause the instrument to amplify and promote that frequency, but the body of the instrument and the air contained within produce the timbre.*

The instrument's body also produces and contributes sound of its own. The resonant frequency of the air chamber can be heard along with the notes generated by the strings. Another component of the overall sound is the tone produced by the soundboard and backboard and the notes to which they are tuned. *The entire sound we hear comes from all of the parts of the instrument, energized by the strings, acting as a whole. Change one part, and the entire instrument will sound differently.*

The contribution of the parts is very easy to prove. Damp the strings on an instrument and tap the soundboard. Listen to the note produced by the air chamber and the overall quality of the tone you hear. Next, remove the damper, strum or bow the instrument, and listen for the sound of the air chamber along with the notes produced by the strings. The components that produce the sound, stimulated by the strings, are what we hear. Repeat this test until you clearly hear the sound of the air chamber along with the strings. We cannot escape the contribution made by each part of the instrument, and we cannot overlook the importance of tuning each component so that it is in harmony with each other component. It is essential to building instruments that sound excellent.

Tuning the air chamber:
An acoustic instrument's air chamber makes several important contributions: a) it provides an air space where compression and rarefaction affect the surrounding air through the apertures; b) it provides external surfaces whose movement affects the surrounding air; c) it is made up of parts, each tuned to various pitches whose sum total, either by coincidence or design, comprises a specific chord that produces the associated "tone color" of the instrument; and d) its space or cubic volume is tuned to a pitch that is heard as part of the whole tone or sound of the instrument which, in turn, defines the character or timbre of that instrument.

The body is an air pump:
Thinking of it simplistically, an acoustic string instrument is an air pump. It generates waves of energy in the form of mildly compressed air. And the air is the medium through which the sound is transmitted. As previously stated, waves of air are compressed (compression) as they move away from the instrument and rarefied (rarefaction) as they return or are drawn back to fill the void caused by the compression. The instrument is the stimulus; the waves of compression and rarefaction are the vehicle. The constant pulsing of air emanating from the instrument is the delivery mechanism of the sound we hear.

Chapter 2, Rationale for Tap Tuning

How sound is created:
The sequence of events that occur in the production of sound from an instrument is: a) the strings are excited by the musician's bowing or picking; b) the strings' energy drives the bridge in an up and down [movable bridge instruments] or rocking motion [fixed bridge instruments]; c) the bridge causes the soundboard to move up and down in various patterns; d) the soundboard's movement causes compression and rarefaction inside the body [and some compression and rarefaction from the outside surface of the soundboard and backboard]; e) changes in pressure are driven through its soundhole(s) [apertures] and off its outer surfaces; f) layers of surrounding air are caused to move in sympathy; and g) the waves of compression and rarefaction reach our eardrums, and we hear the instrument! Of course, all this happens in just a fraction of a second.

Communicating with the surrounding air:
As a soundboard vibrates, it creates regions of compression and rarefaction from its outer surfaces and from within the space enclosed by the soundboard, rim, and backboard. On most acoustic string instruments, about 75% of the instrument's effective power is produced inside the air chamber and emanates from the soundhole(s), with the remaining 25% generated from the outer surface of the soundboard and backboard. (The actual percentages are dependent on the type and design of the instrument.) This becomes quickly apparent when a performer plays into a microphone. If the microphone is pointing toward the soundboard, the amplitude is moderate; if the microphone is directed toward the soundhole(s), the amplitude is substantially increased.

Parts tuned to a pitch:
Each discrete component of an instrument has a resonant frequency of its own. The backboard, when isolated and tapped, produces a tone, and the soundboard produces its own tone. The air chamber (more specifically, its space or cubic volume) has its own resonant frequency. To be effective in producing a balanced tone with good amplitude, each component must be tuned to be in harmony with each other component.

The tuning in harmony is what gives any one instrument its particular sound or voice and distinguishes it from other instruments. For example: let's say we have a guitar with a soundboard tuned to a *C*, an air chamber tuned to an *E*, and a backboard tuned to a *G*. Assuming, for a moment,

13

The Art of Tap Tuning

that they will not change when we put the instrument together, these three notes will produce a *C* chord. The resident *C* chord sound of the body will be present along with every note we play and will be the key element that contributes to the instrument's overall timbre or color and sets it aside from other instruments.

More importantly, the combination of the specific notes to which the various parts are tuned directly affects how the instrument sounds – bright, mellow, warm, happy, sad – as well as those other qualities we attribute to chords and keys. We typically think of the key of *C* being bright and formal, *E* being warm and mellow, and so on. The secret to an instrument's dynamics and timbre comes from properly tuning its parts, and the luthier can tune the various parts to keys that have the desired tonal characteristics. These attributes will then establish the instrument's overall timbre.

When tuning the instrument, it is desirable to find notes that while still part of the *A*440 standard, are notes not common to the keys we play in. Of course, this is impossible to do completely. So, while sharps or flats are found in almost every key, as a general guide it is advisable to tune the soundboard and backboard of the instrument to a note that is either sharp or flat (e.g., *B♭, C♯, A♯*).

As with the soundboard and backboard, the air chamber must be tuned to a note, and much to our chagrin, the instrument comes excessively alive when that note, or more particularly, that chord is played. For example, it is very typical to find "dreadnaught" sized guitars with air chambers tuned to a *G* or *G♯*. When a *G* chord or *G♯* chord is played, the instrument responds more so than it does to any other chord. It just "pops" and this is to due to the resonant frequency of the air chamber being excited by a sympathetic vibration; the stimulus of an identical frequency.

The good news for picked (as opposed to bowed) instruments is that the instrument "pops" only once since it peaks and decays quickly from the singular attack of the pick. On the violin, however, the bowed energy is continuous compared to the singular attack of the pick on the guitar or mandolin. When a note is played on the violin that matches the tuning of the air chamber, the instrument comes alive and resonates more loudly than any other note, and, as previously mentioned, it results in the unwanted "wolf note."

It is interesting to note that sympathetic vibrations can not only wreak havoc on sound, they can also be disastrous elsewhere. In November 1940, the Tacoma Narrows Bridge was subject to severe winds. The pulsing wind blowing against the structure stimulated the resonant frequency of the bridge, which caused massive vibrations to build up in the roadbed. The vibrations became so severe that the structure began to oscillate and finally collapse. Although historical records do not speak to the sounds emanating from the bridge prior to its collapse, there is a good possibility that a massive "wolf note" was howling a death toll.

Determining the right note:
One would think the ideal thing to do is to tune the body off-frequency to avoid the often-played notes. For example, using concert pitch of *A*440, the body could be tuned to 442Hz, a little closer to *A♯* (*A* is 440Hz and *A♯* is 466.16Hz). Unfortunately, that doesn't work because there is a very good possibility that we would hear "beats" that are the difference of the *A*440 note and the body at 442Hz, or 2 beats or pulses per second. But, we could go halfway to, let's say, *A*452 or *A*453 (there is a 26Hz difference between *A*440 and *A♯*466.16) and not hear the beats because at around 12Hz or 13Hz we just begin to lose the separate pulsing "beats." Tuning a quarter tone off will work, but only as long as the music community agrees that *A*=440Hz (see Appendices D and E). If *A* ever becomes 435Hz or 445Hz, it could wreak havoc on instruments tuned a quarter tone off.

Regardless of the note selected, the tuning of the body parts and air chamber must be based on a note that is part of the *A*440 standard (or the standard concert pitch at the time the instrument is built) and not tuned a few cents sharp or flat (to avoid beats).

Mandolin and 12-string guitar players are used to hearing beats, as these instruments feature two strings per note. As the pairs of strings are adjusted to the correct pitch, we can hear the difference between a pair that are almost in tune with each other as a pulsing sound we call "beats." So, when one *A*440 string is in perfect pitch and the partner string is a little sharp, let's say *A*445, the musician will hear the 5 beats (5 pulses per second) difference between the strings (445-440= 5). As the strings get closer in pitch, the beats get slower until they finally go away when the strings are in perfect unison.

Chapter 2, Rationale for Tap Tuning

I cannot emphasize enough that getting all of the components to pitch and getting them to a note that is part of the *A440* scale is critical and plays a vital role in making acoustic string instruments come alive and sound rich.

Note:
Beats can be used to our advantage to add richness to strings. Piano tuners who tune by ear will often apply a technique called "finessing" to impose subtle beats by placing one of the piano's pair or triplet sets just slightly out of tune to give the strings some "color" and keep that note from sounding "cold."

Air chambers tuned to a pitch:
The relationship between the size of air chambers and their resonant frequencies was explored in depth by Hermann (Heinrich von) Helmholtz (1821-1894), a highly respected German scientist. Helmholtz studied the note or pitch that various sized air chambers would produce ("resonant frequencies") when excited using various methods (tapped, picked, bowed, or air blown across the apertures). Helmholtz researched how large chambers produce low notes and how small ones produce high notes. This may seem common place now when we think of low notes of bass viols compared to treble qualities of violins.

Helmholtz also learned that for every chamber size there is an ideally sized aperture (opening) that tunes the chamber and provides maximum amplitude of the chamber's resonant frequency. That is, each air chamber or space has a resonant frequency relative to its size, and each space has an aperture that best tunes that space to an optimum audible level.

It is easy to experiment with these concepts. When we blow across the mouth of a soda bottle, we hear a note that is the resonant frequency of the space in the bottle. If we fill the bottle with water (making the space inside smaller) and blow across the mouth of the bottle, the pitch increases. And, somewhere during the filling process, there is a point where the bottle, with its fixed-size opening, produces tone more loudly than at any other point of being filled. This point is the optimum relationship between the size of the air chamber and the size of the aperture. What happens when we change the size of the opening of the bottle? If we make the opening of the bottle larger, the pitch increases. If we could make the opening smaller, the pitch would decrease. And at some point between the large and the small openings, the bottle would resonate wildly as we achieve a point of maximum amplitude. This maximum amplitude is a result of the opening being the ideal size for the cubic volume of the air chamber it encloses. This relationship is what we seek in tuning the air chamber of musical instruments.

The size of the aperture of an air chamber on a musical instrument should be a result of tuning and not a coincidence of design or construction.

Soundboard loading – the basic premise for tuning:
As previously mentioned, there is a stasis or balance that is reached between the bridge's load on the soundboard and the soundboard's resistance to that load. In both movable and fixed bridge instruments, the resistance of the soundboard is in direct proportion to how stiff the soundboard is, and that stiffness has a direct relationship to how the soundboard is tuned. This is what tap tuning is all about – know something about the tuning, and you know a lot about the stiffness.

The amount of load the bridge exerts on the soundboard is another important issue. The "loading" is a critical element to the amplitude and tonal character of the instrument. A mismatch occurs between the soundboard's rigidity and the bridge's downward pressure or torque load when:

• there is too light a load because the strings pass almost straight over the bridge from the nut to the tailpiece with little or no string break angle, or

• there is too great a load created by a severe string break angle over the bridge, and the soundboard is sent into a visible depression.

The excessive load in the second point cited above constrains the soundboard in its ability to vibrate freely, resulting in the amplitude being greatly reduced. Excessive pressure also raises the pitch of the soundboard beyond the target tunings. And, more importantly, excessive pressure can lead to ruptured braces, soundboards, or both.

For ideal conditions in movable bridge instruments, the proper load is typically achieved by designing the instrument with a 16° to 17° string break angle over the bridge. For fixed bridge instruments, the proper torque can be achieved when the top of the saddle is about 1/2″ above the soundboard, but this is highly dependent on many other factors including size of bridge base and size of bridge

The Art of Tap Tuning

plate. The size of the braces and tone bars are adjusted by the tuning process.

A soundboard deflects under string load. The stiffer the soundboard, the less it deflects. Conversely, the less stiff a soundboard, the more it deflects. And, it follows that a stiffer soundboard produces a higher pitch when tapped, and a less stiff soundboard produces a lower pitch.

The correct balance between soundboard deflection and string load is the outcome of tuning the soundboard by adjusting its stiffness relative to the load of the bridge. Re-read the previous sentence; it is very important.

In this balanced state, the soundboard is in a "ready" position to be instantly responsive to the strings' vibrations. The loading is a critical link in the chain of energy transfer from the strings to the soundboard and from the soundboard to the strings. The better the balance between the soundboard's stiffness and the strings' stiffness (tension), the better the instrument will sound. This also tells us that string gauge and, more specifically, string tension are important components to consider. Changing the strings from one gauge to another changes the way the soundboard is loaded which, in turn, changes the way the instrument responds. In essence, this suggests that a soundboard is (and should be) adjusted for a particular gauge of strings and that changing to a lighter or heavier gauge of strings upsets the balance intended by the designing luthier. (For more information on the tensions of musical strings or selecting string gauges, see *The Luthier's Handbook,* Hal Leonard Corporation, Milwaukee, WI.)

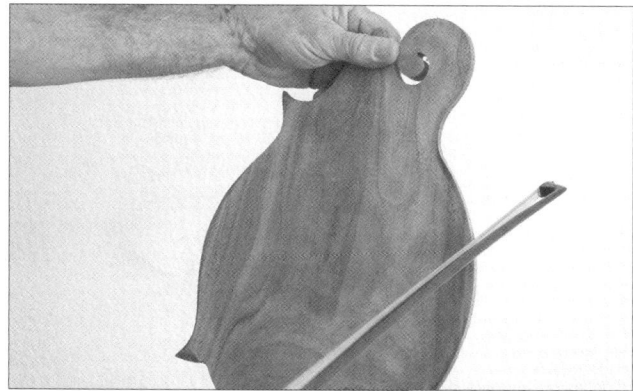

Fig. 2.2 A bow can be drawn along the edge of a free-standing soundboard or backboard to excite its resonant frequency, but the individual tone bars cannot be tuned using the bowing method. If the board is mounted to a rim, the tap method must be used.

Fig. 2.1 This fixture is used to measure how much this Loar-signed F5 mandolin deflects under its string load. If we know the load (see Fig. 1.11) then we can measure how much the soundboard deflects under that load. Therefore, we can tune by deflection as well as by frequency (see Chapter 6, *Production Tuning*).

Note:
In the absence of strobe tuners, Gibson's F5 brochure of 1923 describes its tap tuning process as: *"... each top and back is played on with a bow and struck with a hammer and its pitch determined accurately. The desired pitch is secured by regraduating of the top or back, change in the weight of the tone bars or length of the sound holes – any or all, as may be required. After the instrument is assembled it is strung up and tested before going to the finishing department and if necessary, taken apart and further corrections made in graduation, weight of the tone bars or length of the sound hole."*

The carving of the top and back plates is one of the most critical steps in constructing a violin. As the plates near their desired shapes, the violin-maker tests them by listening to "tap tones." To hear these, the plate is held in a particular way and tapped at a certain spot. The trained ear of the violin maker can extract useful information by noting the pitch and the decay time of the tap tones.
The Science of Sound, Thomas D. Rossing, Addison Wesley Publishing, Reading, MA, 1982

Chapter 3, Factors That Affect the Tuning Process

In this and following chapters, the word "bars" is used in a general sense to refer to either tone bars or braces that are being tuned. "Plates" (the acoustical term for tone-producing components like soundboards) is used to refer to either soundboards or backboards.

Where to tap:
In order to determine the resonant frequency of the part, it must be excited so it begins to vibrate and this is best accomplished by tapping with a soft "hammer."

• The ideal place to tap the soundboard is on the center of each tone bar or brace (from inside the soundboard).
The tone bars and braces are the most rigid components of the soundboard and are the targeted elements to be tuned.

• The ideal place to tap the backboard is on the center. If the back is braced (as in the case of most guitars), tap on the center of each brace.
Plates produce different partials depending on where they are excited. To excite the fundamental, the plate should be struck in its centermost location.

• To tune bridgeplates on acoustic guitars, tap on the center of the bridgeplate.
The stiffness of other structural members is adjusted just as braces and tone bars are. Tuning is the ideal way to adjust the relative stiffness of bridgeplates and cross-grain supports.

• When measuring the resonant frequency of the air chamber in preparation for adjusting the apertures, tap on the center or crown of the soundboard at the location of the bridge. If the instrument is strung, damp the strings and tap on the bridge.
Exciting the fundamental of the air chamber can be best achieved by exciting the entire soundboard.

Soundboard:
The soundboard is tuned by adjusting its stiffness. The first step is to properly establish the soundboard's thickness so that its general mass and stiffness are within range of adjustment. For flat spruce soundboards, this typically calls for a thickness of .110" (2.8mm) to .120" (3.0mm), or for .115" (2.9mm) in the thinnest area of graduated spruce soundboards. The second step is to adjust the tone bars and/or braces.

• Before tuning the soundboard, it should be glued to the rim to anchor it around its perimeter.
A fundamental is best achieved by securing a plate along its edge. Plates produce a different fundamental and partial series when secured around their edges than they do when held free in the air.

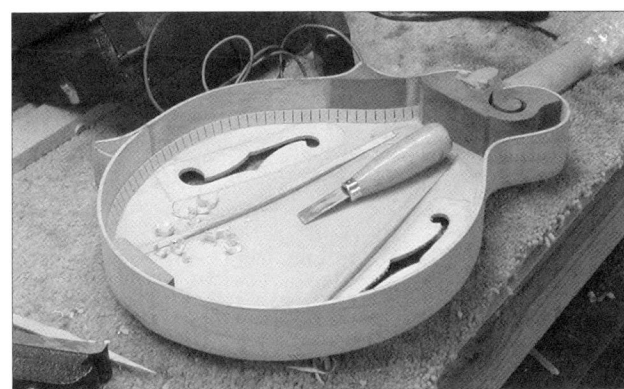

Fig. 3.1 In order to excite the correct fundamental, soundboards should be tuned while attached to the rim.

Tone bars and braces:
Arched and graduated soundboards (mandolin, viol family, arched-top guitars) get their strength and dimensional stability (ability to fight distortion) from the curved shape of the board, not from tone bars affixed to their inner surface. The job of the tone bars is to provide a means for adjusting the soundboard's tuning, not to add strength.

A steel-string acoustic guitar has both braces and tone bars. The braces are structural members and are used to keep the soundboard from deforming under the torque load of the strings. The tone bars also add some strength, but are there primarily to control the tonal behavior of the un-braced region of the soundboard between the bridgeplate and the butt of the instrument.

The Art of Tap Tuning

- Tuning the soundboard is accomplished by removing wood from the bars, by thinning the soundboard, or a combination of both.

As you remove wood from a bar, it becomes less rigid resulting in lowering the frequency. That is, as wood is removed, the note created by the bar becomes lower because the bar and the soundboard to which it is attached become less stiff.

- The pitch to which a bar can be tuned is dependent on the location of the bar. A bar positioned nearer to the center of a soundboard produces a higher pitch than a bar positioned nearer to the edge of a soundboard. (See *Tone bar and brace location*, page 21.)

A plate that is stiffer in the center produces a higher pitch than a similar plate that is stiffer around its periphery.

- Removing wood from the ends of the bar changes the frequency more gradually than removing wood from the center. Conversely, removing wood from the center of the bar changes the frequency more quickly.

Removing wood from the ends of the bar changes its overall mass (weight and size), but only mildly alters the stiffness of the bar. Removing wood from the center of the bar enhances its flexibility while only mildly altering its overall mass.

- Removing wood from the sides of the bar changes the tuning more slowly than removing wood from the height of the bar.

Removing wood from the sides of the bar helps to reduce mass (weight and size) without having a major impact on the bar's stiffness. Removing wood from the sides of the bar is an ideal way to fine-tune the bar.

- Wood removed from both the ends and the center of a bar in two distinct steps, will leave small peaks near each end that is suggestive of "scalloped" bracing.

Other than the singular peaked scallop on the bass bar directly below the bridge on viol-family instruments, scalloped braces do not appear to have a significant acoustical attribute. The viol family features this peak to evenly transition the soundboard's stiffness away from the bridge.

- Removing wood from one bar will have an affect on the tuning of the other bar. Roughly shape both bars first to what feels right for your construction, and then tune each bar slowly and carefully, removing wood from one bar and then from the other bar. Continue to re-check the tuning of the bars as you proceed. Do not tune one bar fully and then attempt to tune the other bar – alternate tuning the bars.

Everything in the instrument's structure is part of a coupled system in which each part interacts with, and has an affect on, the other parts.

- The final shape of a bar is the outcome of tuning and not a result of design.

The design aspect is taken into consideration in the initial shaping of the bar (as in the scalloped braces of some acoustic steel-string guitars and the single-peaked viol-family bass bar). The lasting and final shape of the bar should be a result of tuning and stiffness adjustments.

Backboard:
As with the soundboard, the backboard is tuned by adjusting its stiffness. Carved backboards without braces can be adjusted by thinning the boards (usually from the inside). If the backboard has braces (i.e., acoustic guitar), the braces can be adjusted in a manner similar to the tone bar adjustment.

The backboard should be attached to a fixture so it is secure around its perimeter. Fig. 3.2 shows a fixture for mandolin backboards, but a similar fixture can be built for any style instrument. Clamps should be positioned to accept either soundboards or backboards so that the plate can be tuned separately from the rim, if desired. (See Fig. 5.1)

- For an arched and graduated backboard, removing wood from the crown of the backboard will

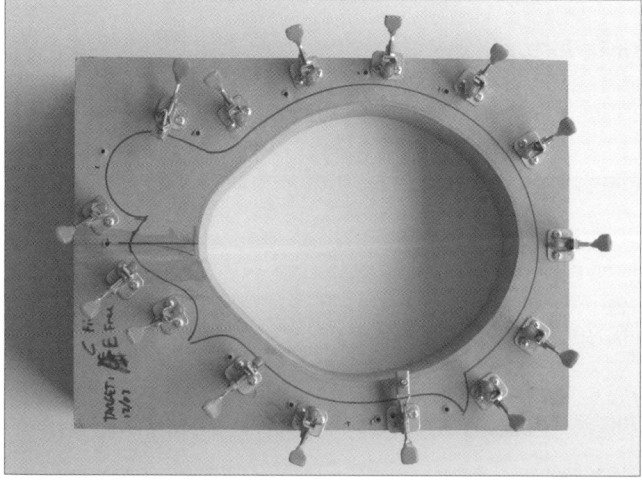

Fig. 3.2 For the tuning process, the backboard should be attached around its perimeter and, therefore, must be off the instrument. This fixture is used to hold a mandolin backboard and has toggle clamps to enable the quick attachment and release of the backboard.

Chapter 3, Factors That Affect the Tuning Process

change the frequency quickly. Removing wood from the minimum area (the thin area that runs almost all the way around the backboard) will change the frequency slowly.

As with braces and tone bars, a backboard's overall stiffness is more rapidly modified by removing wood from its center than from its edges.

Note:
If you attach the backboard first and the soundboard last, as some luthiers do in guitar construction, you can tune the backboard after it is attached to the rim, and tune the soundboard by attaching it to a support fixture.

Apertures:

To visualize how apertures work, imagine you have an adjustable aperture on your instrument. As you keep closing the aperture (and the pitch lowers), you reach a point where there is too much restriction (opening is too small) for compression and rarefaction to be effective. At this point, the amplitude quickly begins to suffer. If you go further, you arrive at a point where the air chamber is cut off from the surrounding air and can only generate sound pressure (waves of compression and rarefaction) from the front surface of the soundboard or back surface of the backboard. At this point, the instrument will sound "dead" or muffled and will lack any projection quality.

Going the other way, as the aperture gets larger, the pitch raises. As you keep enlarging the aperture, you reach a point where the ability to create controlled levels of compression and rarefaction is reduced. At this point, the instrument has more power than one with a restricted or closed soundhole, but will sound "thin" and lack warmth or timbre. An instrument with an excessively large soundhole lacks power and richness; and like the instrument with a restricted soundhole, it lacks projection.

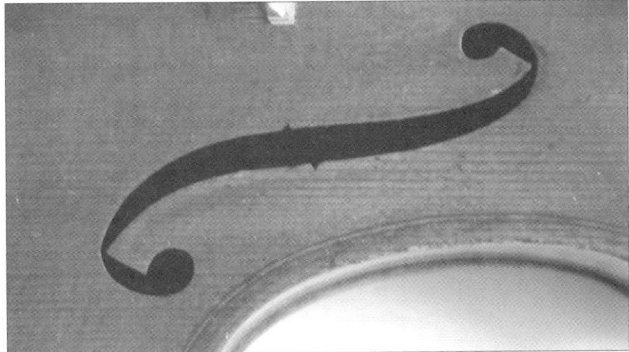

Fig. 3.3 The *f*-hole apertures of this violin control the tuning of the air chamber as well as the level of compression and rarefaction the instrument can generate.

If the aperture(s) continue to be enlarged beyond this "excessively large" point, the ability to create compression and rarefaction is lost completely and the amplitude radically drops further.

Although an air chamber can be tuned by changing the size of the aperture(s), it is important to remember that *for every given air chamber size there is a specific aperture size that best tunes that space.* That is, there is an ideally sized opening that makes the air chamber most resonant.

• Within the previously stated guidelines, the size of aperture(s) affects the tuning of the chamber to which it is attached.
As the size of the aperture <u>increases</u>, the resonant frequency of the air chamber increases. As the size of the aperture of the air chamber <u>decreases</u>, the resonant frequency of the air chamber decreases.

Air chamber:

The air chamber establishes the resonant frequency of the instrument and provides an enclosure within which compression and rarefaction take place.

• The size of the air chamber determines the resonant frequency of its space. The pitch associated with every air chamber is due to the difference in wave lengths that can be achieved within each space. The massive bodies (air chambers) of the bass viols are designed to enhance their low notes; the relatively small bodies of violins are sized to enhance their higher notes.
As the cubic volume of the air chamber <u>increases</u>, the resonant frequency decreases. As the cubic volume of the air chamber <u>decreases</u>, the resonant frequency increases.

• The shape of the air chamber has an effect on the timbre on the instrument. (Oblong vs round, flat soundboard and backboard vs arched soundboard and backboard.)
While the shape of the air chamber affects the voice and timbre of the instrument, it has little bearing on its tuning (unless the shape is a radical departure, has multiple discrete bouts, etc.) and is, therefore, not within the scope of this text.

General tap tuning facts:

• Stiffness is one factor that affects frequency, and as previously mentioned, it becomes immediately apparent when one considers the process of tuning musical instrument strings. As the strings are

The Art of Tap Tuning

tightened up to pitch, the tension increases, and as the strings are made more stiff, the frequency of the string increases. Conversely, as the strings are slackened, tension decreases (strings made less stiff), the frequency of the string decreases.
As the stiffness of a component increases, the resonant frequency of the component increases. As the stiffness decreases, the resonant frequency of the component decreases.

• Composition is related to stiffness. Woods with more tightly integrated cellular structure (i.e., smaller pores) typically have a denser composition. Maple is more dense than pine, and it contains more crystallized glucose than pine with the result that it weighs more per cubic foot. The cell walls of maple are smaller and stiffer than those in pine, and this results in a stiffer piece of wood than a piece of pine of the same size. Similarly, Douglas Fir is heavier than other members of the *Pinaceae* family because of its higher cell and wood tar density. The greater the density, the higher its resonant frequency.
As the material's composition becomes more dense and stiff, the component's resonant frequency increases. As the composition becomes less dense and stiff, the component's resonant frequency decreases.

The very nature of wood dictates that every piece of wood of the same species is different from the next; tree to tree, board to board, inch by inch. The specific weight of woods of the same species can vary by as much as 10%. This differential dictates that soundboards and backboards should be tuned and cannot just be carved to a predetermined thickness or graduation.

• Mass is a term that describes an object's weight and size taken as a whole. By definition, mass relates to an object's ability to overcome inertia and how much energy is required to set it in motion.
As an object's mass increases, the resonant frequency decreases. As mass decreases, the resonant frequency increases.

Because mass relates to size, there is an inverse relationship to frequency. The larger an object (i.e., the more mass it has), typically the lower the resonant frequency it produces. This is immediately apparent with musical strings, for it is here that wrap wire is added to the bass strings to increase their mass and, as a result, lowers their frequency.

Another good example is the xylophone. The bars that produce the lower notes are larger than the bars that produce the higher notes. And, in the case of the xylophone, the bars are all the same composition.

• It is a matter of physics that a plate vibrates differently when held free in the air compared to when held around the edges. The plate held free can have either nodes or anti-nodes along its edges. That is, the edges or perimeter of the plate can be in either a state of vibration or rest according to the note or pitch to which it is vibrating, and this is entirely dependent on whether the plate is secured around its edges or not.
Plates affixed to a rim will tune a fourth higher than plates held free in the air. Therefore, a backboard that is tuned to an E free in the air will be an A (a fourth above the E) when it is anchored around its edges.

• Soundboards and backboards measured free in the air will be the same amount *sharp* or *flat* as when attached to the rim (although the note will be higher). For example, if you measure a soundboard that produces E164.81+25 cents (3rd octave E) when held free in the air, it will produce an A220+25 cents (3rd octave A) when clamped into a fixture and held by its rim. The note is higher, but it is the same 25 cents sharp. (A "cent" is 100th of a semitone.)
Whether a plate is secured around its edge or held free in the air, it will produce a note that has the same sharp or flat qualities.

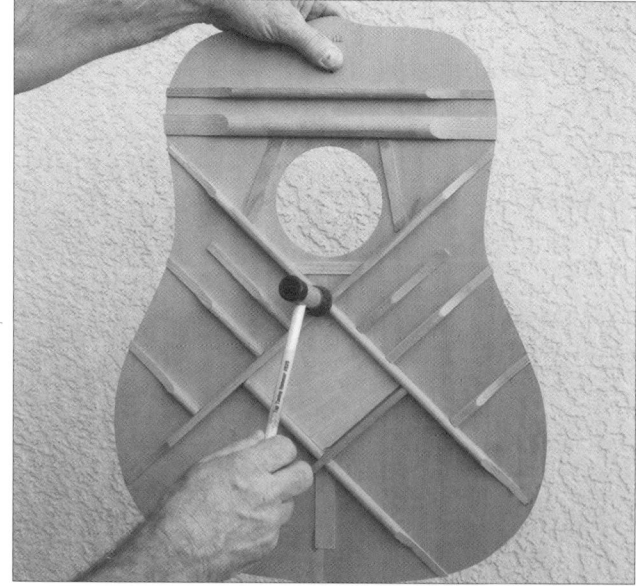

Fig. 3.4 A plate held free in the air vibrates in different modes than a plate held around its perimeter.

Chapter 3, Factors That Affect the Tuning Process

Tone bar and brace location:
The location of a brace or tone bar affects the tuning of the soundboard. As a brace or tone bar is positioned closer to the center of a soundboard, the pitch increases. Conversely, as a brace or tone bar is positioned closer to the edge of a soundboard, the pitch decreases.

Soundboards can be braced symmetrically or asymmetrically. The soundboard of a violin, for example, is asymmetrically braced having only a "bass bar" and no treble bar. The bass bar is positioned to the bass side of the soundboard and aligned so that it transverses directly beneath the bass foot of the bridge. (As described in Chapter 1, a sound post is used to support the bridge on the treble side of the violin, act as a fulcrum to drive energy to the bass bar, and couple the plates.)

The F5 style mandolin, designed by Lloyd Loar in 1922, has two asymmetrical tone bars (Fig. 3.5) with the bass bar positioned closer to the bass *f*-hole and the treble bar positioned and aligned more closely to the centerline of the instrument.

Acoustic steel string guitars typically feature braces positioned in an "X" with the braces intersecting below the soundhole, with at least one or two transverse (cross) braces above the soundhole. The accompanying tone bars are either symmetrical or asymmetrical according to the design and manufacturer. The X-brace design plays a vital role in stiffening the soundboard and counteracting the torque force of the bridge from the steel strings that develop anywhere from 125 to 175 pounds of load (according to gauge).

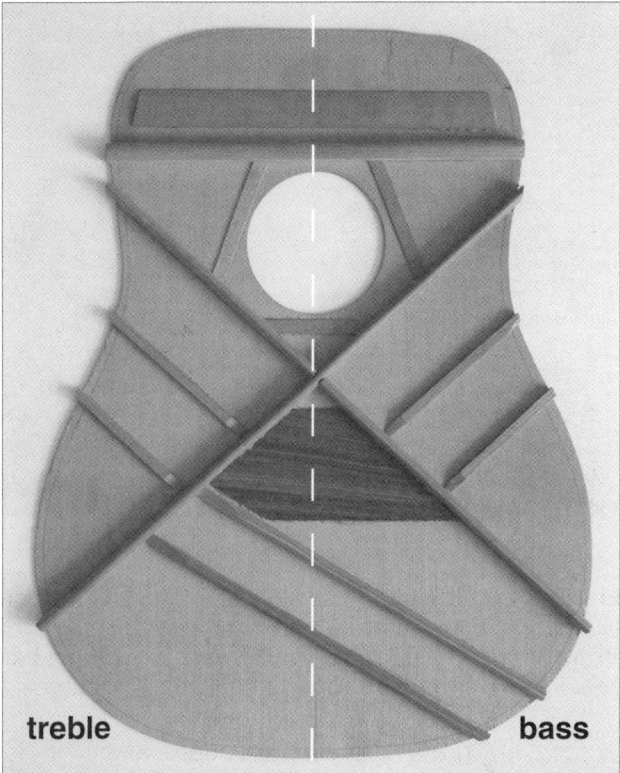

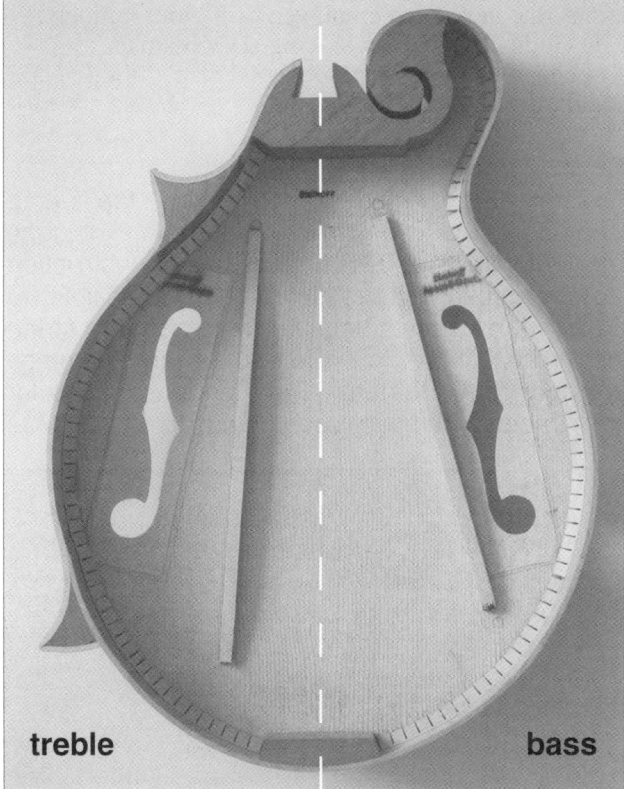

Fig. 3.5 The tone bars on this F5 mandolin soundboard are positioned asymmetrically enabling them to be more easily tuned to different notes.

Fig. 3.6 Christian F. Martin (1796-1873) is credited with the development of the X-bracing system. This unfinished Martin soundboard from 1985 shows two symmetrical X braces, four side braces, two diagonal tone bars, and a rosewood bridge plate.

Classical guitars typically feature a few cross braces with the tone bars laid out in a pattern that the Spanish refer to as *barretas abanicas* or "fan bracing." The lighter load of the classical guitar's nylon strings (about 80 pounds) allows a more delicate bracing configuration.

Smaller instruments with round or oval soundholes such as an A-model mandolin, Florentine mandolin, balalaika, pandorina, and lute commonly have a single cross brace running either partially or entirely across the width of the soundboard.

Grand pianos, harpsichords, spinets, and other instruments with massive soundboards most commonly have an array of parallel braces running

The Art of Tap Tuning

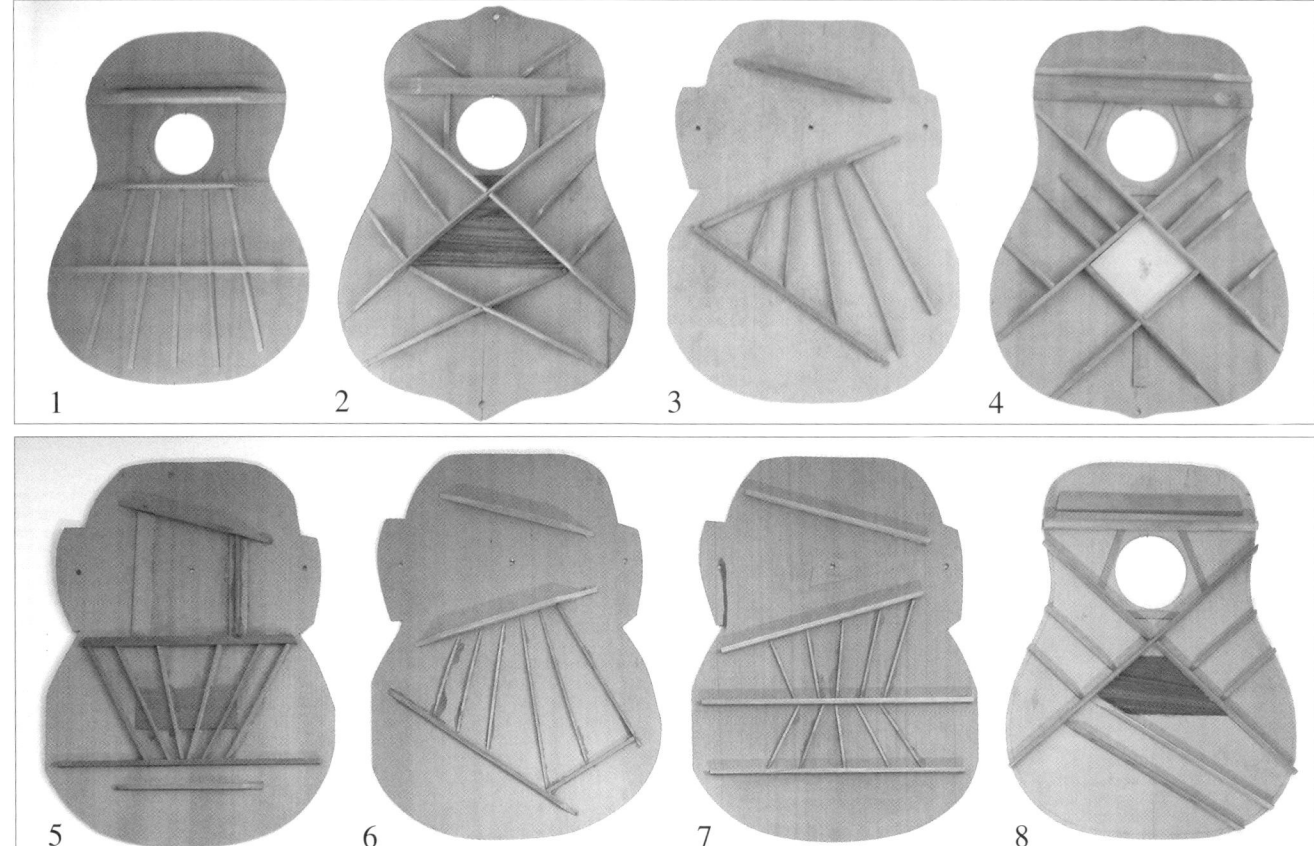

Fig. 3.7 It is difficult to reference all of the bracing configurations that have been employed by various builders, but these eight soundboards are examples of some variations. 1) Guild classical fan bracing. 2) Mossman steel string modified X-bracing. 3) Ovation classical fan bracing. 4) Gibson double-X with plywood maple bridge plate. 5, 6, and 7) Ovation classical fan bracing (variations). 8) Martin X-bracing.

across the grain of the soundboard at an angle that best suits the design and shape of the piano and its soundboard (Fig. 3.9).

Regardless of the symmetry or location, tone bars and braces should be: 1) tuned to either the same note as each other or to notes that are a half- or whole-step apart; and 2) tuned to a note of the concert pitch in use (e.g., *A440* in 2007).

Target tunings:

This text is designed to describe the tap tuning technique. The vast array of instrument designs coupled with a wide combination of construction features make it impractical, if not impossible, to provide the target tunings for every acoustic string instrument. I have provided some target tunings in Appendix C. To determine the ideal tunings for instruments you build, you should:

Fig. 3.8 This 1918 Gibson A1 mandolin features a single cross brace below the soundhole.

Fig. 3.9 The soundboard of this upright piano features numerous parallel braces.

Chapter 3, Factors That Affect the Tuning Process

1. Build a test instrument of the style and construction that you plan to replicate.

2. Keep making changes, experimenting with: soundhole(s) size, shape, and location; soundboard stiffness and wood species; soundboard and backboard thicknesses; and brace and tone bar size and shape until the instrument has the desired timbre. (This is the hard part.)

3. Measure the resonant frequency of the air chamber using the tap tuning procedures described in Chapters 4 and 5.

4. Remove the backboard, and measure the resonant frequencies of the backboard, soundboard, and all the braces and/or tone bars using the procedures described in Chapters 4 and 5.

For example, if you are building an F5 mandolin, you might learn that it is optimum to have the bass bar at $G\sharp$ ($A\flat$), the treble bar at $A\sharp$ ($B\flat$), the backboard at C, and the air chamber at $D\sharp$.

The affects of finishes on tuning:
Applications of 10 to 12 coats of lacquer finish do not greatly affect the tuning, but does have an affect on the overall timbre of the instrument – making it brighter. This is especially true when acrylic lacquer or polyester finishes are used. If you are interested in learning more about the affects of finishes as they relate to tuning and what happens as you apply more coats of finish, these are described in great detail in *The Luthier's Handbook* (Hal Leonard Corporation, Milwaukee, WI).

Reference tuning:
The tone emitted from a tapped bar, soundboard, backboard, or air chamber is unique and its timbre is unlike the tone generated by a string, tuning fork, or other tone-emitting device. In the tap tuning process there are basically two objectives: 1) arriving at the correct tuning with great precision; and 2) repeating the process with subsequent instruments.

Strobe tuners play a vital role in arriving at the correct, final tuning. However, making gross tuning steps – major adjustments leading up to the fine tuning – also can be facilitated by having a reference part close at hand for comparative audible tests. For example, tap a tuned backboard (with a known tuning value) next to a to-be-tuned backboard; a known (tuned) air chamber next to a to-be-tuned air chamber, and so on. In this process, hearing tones with similar timbre makes it easier to distinguish between the tuning of the two parts. If you tap one backboard and then tap another, it becomes immediately evident which of the boards is tuned to a higher or lower pitch. In the absence of strobe tuners, the early luthiers used reference tuning to build their production instruments.

Notes:
1) Make copies of Appendix A so that you can keep a record of the tuning process.

2) Appendix C provides a list of 12 common target tunings. We will attempt to build this list over time and will provide an appendix update in our web site at *www.siminoff.net*. We welcome your contributions to this list – please email them to *siminoff@siminoff.net*.

3) Developing a solid set of target tunings comes from building one or two instruments with measurable tuning values. To facilitate building wood-bodied acoustic string test instruments, you can use a paper shim between the backboard and the rim (Fig. 3.10) when the backboard is glued on. Then, if the backboard needs to be removed for additional tests or adjustments, the paper shim can be easily sliced through with a razor blade for simple removal of the backboard.

Fig. 3.10 A thin paper shim can be glued between the backboard and the rib/lining to facilitate removal of the backboard for stringing and testing. This test mandolin has been opened a dozen or more times to modify the bracing of its four-piece soundboard.

An enclosed mass of air, like that of the violin, viola, and violincello, bounded by elastic plates, has certain proper tones which may be evoked by blowing across the openings or 'f-holes.'
<u>On the Sensations of Tone</u>, Hermann Helmholtz, Dover Publications, Inc.
New York City, 1954 (first published in 1877)

Chapter 4, Preparation for Tuning

The tuning process:
There are three basic components of the tuning process:

1) Tuning the soundboard by adjusting each of the braces and/or tone bars after the soundboard is attached to the rim, but before the instrument is fully assembled.

2) Tuning the backboard by adjusting its stiffness (a result of adjusting its thickness or cross braces in the case of a guitar) before the instrument is assembled.

3) Tuning, and then voicing the aperture(s) after the instrument has been assembled.

Methods of tuning:
Stiffness and frequency are closely related. Therefore, soundboards and backboards can be tuned by measuring either their frequency or their stiffness. Frequency tuning calls for exciting (tapping or bowing) a part of the instrument, measuring the pitch to which it is tuned, and then changing the stiffness of that part to adjust the tuning.

Tapping requires the use of a soft-faced "hammer," which tends to reduce the number of partials produced and primarily excites the fundamental. Bowing uses a viol-family bow, drawing it across the edge of the backboard or soundboard to excite it into vibration. While bowing produces a strong and easily measured note, it can only be done on disassembled parts and cannot be used to measure the differences in various individual tone bars or braces. The tap hammer can be used on all parts of the instrument and is preferred over the bowing method because it can be used on partially or completely assembled parts. Therefore, this text focuses primarily on the tap tuning method.

Deflection tuning is a process I developed in the mid-1970s, driven by the need to work in noisy production environments. Stiffness of a correctly tuned part is determined by measuring how much the part deflects under a specific load. Then, to achieve the desired consistency of subsequent production parts, the braces and tone bars are subjected to a pre-determined load and shaved – which alters their stiffness – until the deflection of the new part matches the deflection of the correctly tuned part.

Deflection tuning cannot be used for adjusting the air chamber's tuning. The air chamber of the instrument can only be tuned by exciting the space within and measuring the note it produces. The adjustment is made to the apertures until the optimum opening is determined for that given air chamber.

Frequency (tap) tuning and deflection tuning are inextricably connected and both have the final outcome of adjusting a part's stiffness. However, for deflection tuning, a correctly tuned part must first be achieved through the frequency (tap) tuning method before measurements can be taken.

Tap tuning requires working in a rather quiet environment with minimal background noise from sanders, planers, or other extraneous noise. Deflection tuning, therefore, is more efficient in noisy production environments because it uses mechanical measurement and is not affected by ambient sounds or noise.

See *Chapter 6, Production Tuning* for more information on deflection tuning. (For a full description of the deflection tuning process see *The Luthier's Handbook*, Hal Leonard Corporation, Milwaukee, WI.)

Adjusting the air chamber:
Tuning the air chamber is fundamentally dependent on the air chamber's size. As the air chamber is made larger, its resonant frequency is lowered. As the air chamber is made smaller, its resonant frequency is made higher. The fine tuning of the air chamber is accomplished by adjusting the size of the aperture(s).

Air chamber *size* is a design feature. With the exception of post-construction adjustments that can

Chapter 4, Preparation for Tuning

be made to the size of the cavity of resonator-type banjos, air chamber size is not something that is readily adjustable on an in-construction or finished instrument.

Tap hammers:
The art of building padded hammers dates back to the piano actions first demonstrated by Bartolommeo Cristofori in 1709. The hammers were made of wood, covered in leather, and built up with several layers of felt, each of a different density. The goal was to excite the string without imparting to it a particular partial or partial series.

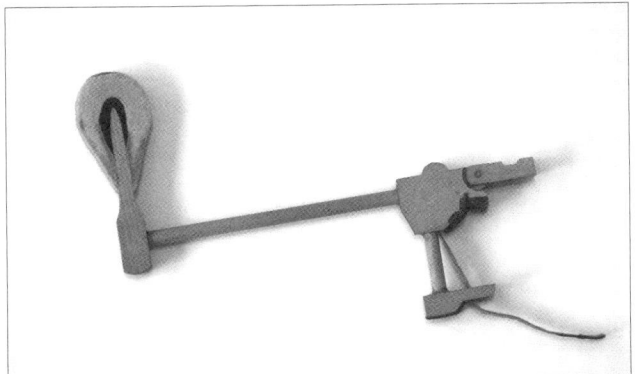

Fig. 4.1 Piano hammers feature delicately crafted heads that are shaped to a point, covered with multiple layers of felt of various densities.

There are several ways to construct a tap tune hammer. The head should be light weight and the face of the hammer covered with several layers of cloth or felt.

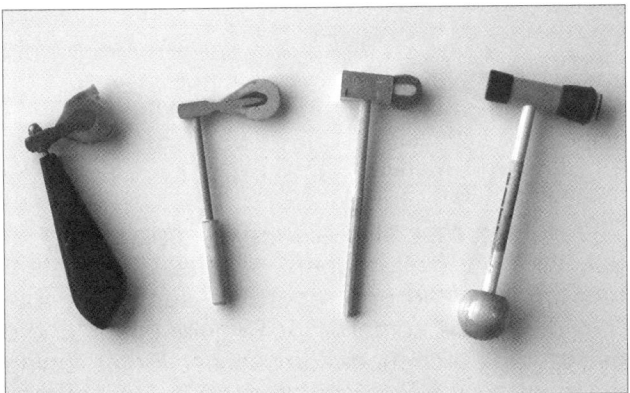

Fig. 4.2 Tap tune hammers should have light weight heads with felt-padded faces. The ball handle on the commercial tap hammer (right) allows the hammer to roll in the palm of the hand for consistent taps.

Note:
Protect your hammer from damage and ensure that the felt head stays clean and does not get contaminated with adhesives, liquids, debris, sharp filings, etc.

Why strobe tuners for tap tuning?
Regular digital tuners (those that don't have spinning discs but use either digital [i.e., numerical] readouts or a moving needle/arm) are great for tuning strings and instruments that have sustain. However, for tap tuning, a tuner is needed that will provide an instantaneous response. Here's why:

When a <u>string</u> is excited (Fig. 4.3), the initial "attack" is followed by several seconds of continued vibrational modes of the string that are the result of the relationship between the energy of the attack and the energy stored in the string (because the string is at tension). There is some additional sustain caused by the restoring force. However, when a <u>body or object</u> is tapped – as in tap tuning a violin or mandolin soundboard, or tuning a drum head – the attack is abrupt, followed by very little sustain (Fig. 4.4). In essence, we say that the tapped tone has a fast peak and a fast decay.

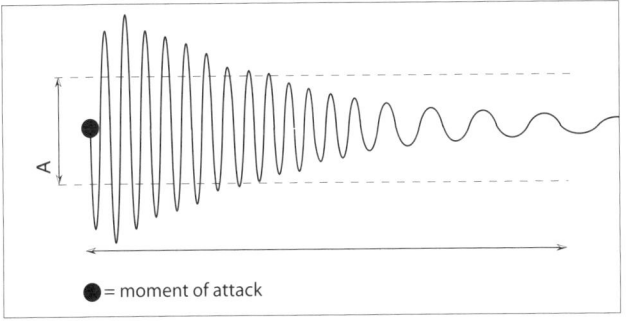

Fig. 4.3 When a string is picked or plucked, the vibrations continue for a long period of time because of the elasticity of the wire, the tension of the string, and the restoring force of the soundboard or membrane to which it is attached.

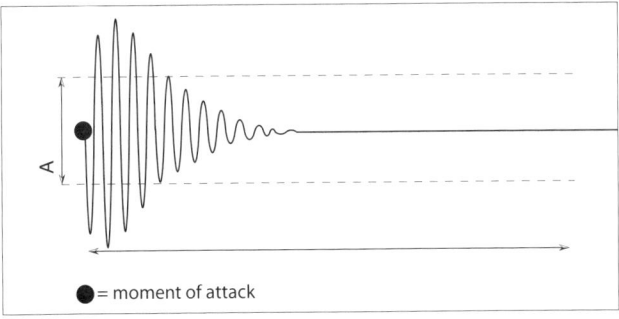

Fig. 4.4 When a soundboard or backboard is tapped, the vibrational modes decay quickly because there is significant damping and no restoring force.

What separates "true mechanical" strobe tuners from other analog or digital tuners are as follows:

1. Tuners without a true stroboscopic display have to choose between fundamental and overtone

The Art of Tap Tuning

signals which, in a complex signal, can be of similar amplitude. The true mechanical strobe tuner shows all components of the signal without having to select one.

2. Digital tuners do not operate in real-time. They are designed to take several samples during the first few seconds of the string's sustain, calculate the data, and report the results to a digital or LED display. However, since there is no significant sustain in tap tuning, regular digital tuners cannot read and report the information quickly enough to be accurate. By the time a regular digital tuner can sample the signal of a tapped tone, the signal of the tap tuned object has decayed.

For tap tuning, we need a device capable of measuring and reporting the initial attack and displaying this information instantly.

Selecting a tuner:
The ideal tuners for tap tuning are the earlier analog devices made by both Peterson and Conn (Conn is now part of Peterson ElectroMusical). These systems have mechanical wheels that spin in front of a strobe light and use analog (as opposed to digital) circuitry. These analog systems, typically favored by piano tuners are no longer made today, and the best place to find them is on the used market (check with a local piano store).

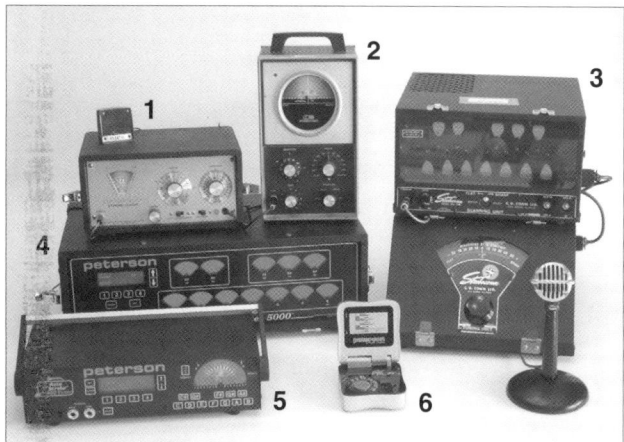

Fig. 4.5 Generations of tuners: 1) Peterson 400 (ca 1975). 2) C.G.Conn ST-11 (ca 1980). 3) C.G.Conn 6T5 multi-wheel with manual tune (lower unit) (ca 1972). 4) Peterson 5000 multi-wheel (ca 2006). 5) Peterson 490 (ca 2005). 6) Peterson "FLIP" (ca 2006). The first five systems have spinning wheels, and the "FLIP" is a fully digital system with digital display.

Setting up the tuner:
Place the tuner on your workbench so that it is in plain view and the controls are easily accessible. If the unit has a built-in microphone, plug in a remote microphone to the INPUT port to avoid interference from the system's internal motor. Ensure all ambient noise is reduced to an absolute minimum. Things like air compressors, air conditioners, fans, and machinery running in nearby locations can be enough to reduce the accuracy of the information on the strobe tuner.

Using a compressor:
As previously mentioned, the note of a tapped tone has a quick spike and decay. An excellent way to extend that note and obtain a better reading on the strobe tuner is to use a "compressor." A compressor is an electronic device that guitarists use to alter the sustain of a note. The name "compressor" is somewhat misleading because the result is an expanded rather than compressed note. (Actually, a compressor limits the dynamic range of a signal.) Most compressors will expand the sustain of the tapped tone to about a 1.5 or 2 second period, which is sufficient for the strobe tuner to really lock on to the note and report a good image. (See Fig. 4.10).

Fig. 4.6 Compressors are available in many makes, models, and price ranges. Most have controls to adjust the level, attack, and sustain. From left to right; Behringer CS100, Marshall ED-1, Ibanez CP9, and Ibanez Soundtank CP5.

The compressor also allows the opportunity to use the new digital tuners because the system has time to read and report the sustained note provided by the compressor. Regular guitar tuners can be used with moderate success for tap tuning in conjunction with a compressor, but you should test the compressor/tuner combination before you make the purchase. However, most guitar tuners measure only *E, B, G, D,* and *A*.

Connecting the compressor to the tuner is simple; the microphone plugs into the compressor and the compressor plugs into the tuner. All you need is the compressor and one short patch cord.

Chapter 4, Preparation for Tuning

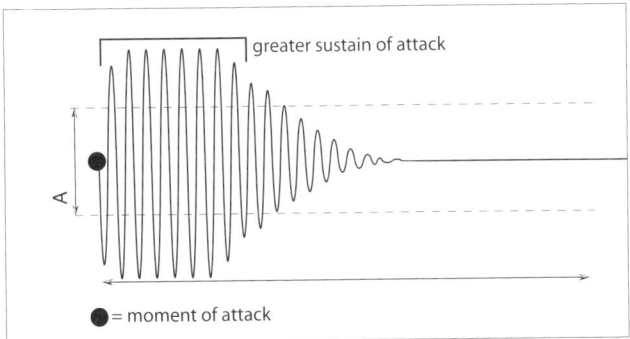

Fig. 4.7 The compressor creates a sustained note and provides the tuner with more time to read and respond. Compare this image of a compressed signal to the relatively short sustain in Figs. 4.3 and 4.4.

In mid-2005, Peterson ElectroMusical released a software version of its digital/mechanical tuners called StroboSoft.™ StroboSoft runs on either the Macintosh or Windows® platform and features a wide array of tools for analyzing musical tones.

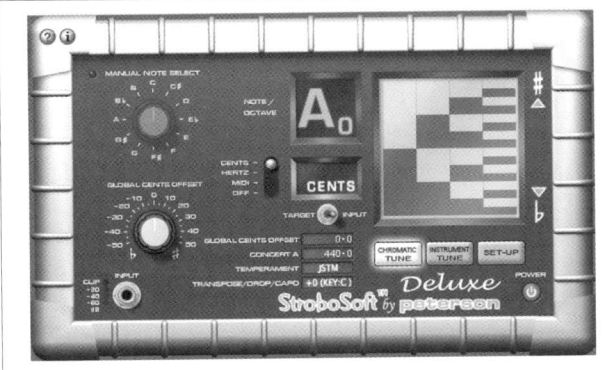

Fig. 4.8 The StroboSoft display provides user-friendly on-screen controls with very responsive read-outs, especially when connected through a compressor.

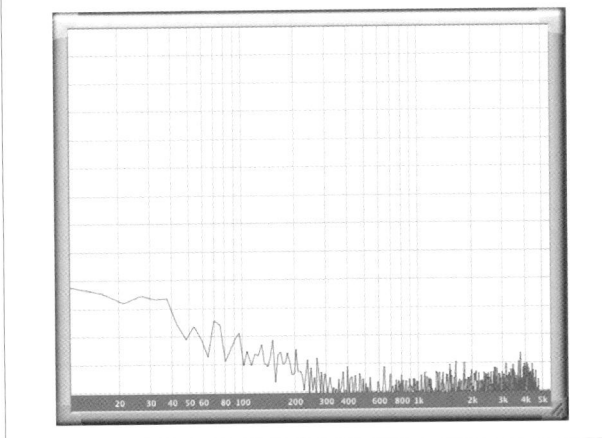

Fig. 4.9 A key feature of the StroboSoft application is the "spectrum window" that displays the intensity and frequency components of a signal in real-time.

In addition to the main control window, the system provides a "spectrum window" that shows the intensity and frequency of the many components (partials) of a musical tone. In combination with a compressor, StroboSoft is an excellent tool (in place of a strobe tuner) to display the tapped notes of tone bars, soundboards, and backboards.

Interpreting the tapped tone:
The first step in the process of learning tap tuning is to be able to recognize and interpret the tapped tone. To this end, I have provided samples of the tapped tones in the companion DVD. The quality of this tone is easier to hear than to describe so it is something you need to try. The test is quite simple – grasp a part along its edge and hold it in the air. Using a tap tune hammer, tap in the center of the part and listen for the note. Hum the note. Repeat the tapping/humming process again. Now, you can: a) hum that note and compare it to a note from a piano, guitar, or other instrument; or b) hum the note into the microphone connected to your tuner. Tap/hum/find is the easiest way to find your first note.

Ideally, you will be able to find the note easily on the tuner. Some new tuners (such as StroboSoft and some of the Peterson strobe tuner models) have an automatic note selection feature that determines what the note is, displays the note on an LCD screen, and switches the wheel to the corresponding speed. On older style tuners that don't have the capability of automatic note selection, you might have to hunt for the note by tapping on the bar or soundboard and turning the note selection dial on the tuner until you arrive at the most vivid image on the wheel (see Fig. 4.10). On manual systems, you may find it advantageous to have an assistant nearby who can turn the dial while you are tapping on the part. To find the note, it is necessary to tap several times about one second apart (a little bit less often if you are using a compressor). Gentle, steady taps are best.

Reading the tuner:
For spinning-wheel tuners, the ideal image is where the wheel appears to stop. The bars closest to the center or hub of the wheel are the lower octaves. The bars closer to the outer edge of the wheel are the upper octaves. The goal is to find the most vivid image at the lowest octave. This image represents the fundamental or resonant frequency of the part being excited. Once you have determined this note and see it on the wheel,

The Art of Tap Tuning

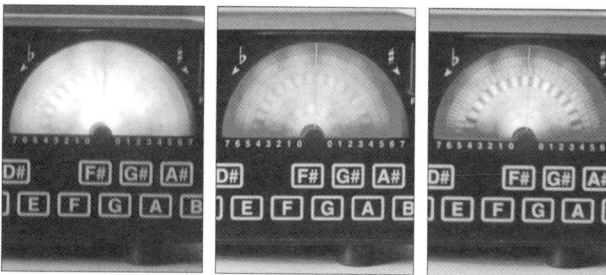

Fig. 4.10 Octaves, partials, and noise are displayed along with the fundamental. These samples show three qualities of the disc display analyzed by the tuner: very questionable (left), possible (center), absolute (right).

you will be able to watch the wheel change as you make adjustments to the part being tuned.

When the wheel appears to stop, the note you are searching for has been found. If the wheel appears to turn slowly clockwise, the note is sharp, and if it appears to turn slowly counter clockwise, the note is flat. The faster it turns, the more sharp or more flat the note is.

You may see other faint images on the wheel; these are either partials or background noise from the room, microphone, electronics, etc.

Changes you will discover:
Heavy or stiff parts may necessitate significant physical changes before they register a change in the pitch. In the case of tone bars, braces, soundboards, and backboards, removing wood lowers the resonant frequency. As you remove wood, you will eventually notice the disc turning counter clockwise indicating that the wood is becoming less stiff and its resonant frequency is dropping. With repeated wood removal, the disc will begin turning faster in a counter clockwise direction indicating that the pitch of the part being tuned has become extremely flat. At this point, you need to switch the tuner to the next lower note so you can read the lower note from a standpoint of how sharp it is. For example, let's assume you are tuning a tone bar and are seeking a perfect A♯, and at the moment, the bar is showing B. As you remove wood from the bar and measure its frequency the wheel begins to spin counter clockwise to indicate that the B is moving toward B♭. Because there are only 100 steps per note, you will eventually get to B -50. At this point, you need to switch to A♯ on the tuner and begin to read the note as A♯ +50. In essence, you are stepping carefully from one half tone to the next.

Test plates:
Before working on valuable soundboards, it is advisable to construct a few test plates with a single tone bar (Fig. 4.11). You can experiment with shaping the tone bars and watching the changes on the tuner. You can use any kind of wood for the surrogate soundboards and tone bars.

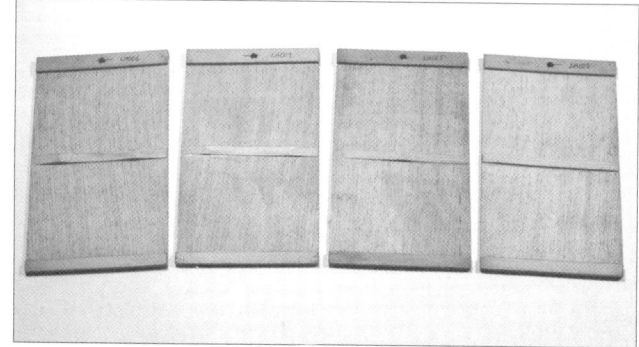

Fig. 4.11 These test "soundboards" were cut from the same board of spruce and are all the same size and thickness, but the tone bars in the center of each one had to be shaped differently to tune the plates to the same note.

Documenting your work:
Make a copy of the tuning record in Appendix A. Use this form to record your tuning procedures so that you have a history of your progress. The document will help provide you with guidelines for repeatability when tuning your future instruments.

Notes:
1) If you keep making changes to the part, but the tuner does not appear to indicate a change in pitch, it is possible that you accidentally determined an incorrect starting point.

2) The description of these products does not constitute an endorsement, nor does it suggest that these are the only products of this type available at the time this text was written.

3) While it is not the goal of this text to evaluate products, the tests I conducted with StroboSoft proved to be excellent. For these tests, I used StroboSoft, a Behringer compressor model CS100, an inexpensive cardioid microphone, running on a pre-Intel Apple G5 Macintosh tower.

4) Since digital technology changes at a rapid pace, this equipment may not be available or it may be superseded by improved models during the life of this publication. I will endeavor to provide current "best practices and tools" in my web site under the "virtual content" page associated with this book. For more information, visit www.siminoff.net.

5) In the absence of electronic tuning equipment, the notes from tapped tones can be compared to notes on any other musical instrument (i.e., piano, organ, guitar).

The theoretical membrane is a perfectly flexible and infinitely thin lamina of solid matter, of uniform material and thickness, which is stretched in all directions by a tension too great as to remain sensibly unaltered during the vibrations and displacements contemplated.
The Theory of Sound, John William Strutt and Lord Baron Rayleigh, Dover Publications, New York, 1945

Chapter 5, Tuning and Voicing

Now that you have the background on how these acoustical systems work and how their resonant frequencies can be adjusted, let's venture into the actual process of tuning and voicing.

There are four simple steps:
1) Tune the soundboard by adjusting its bars.
2) Tune the backboard by adjusting its thickness.
3) Tune the air chamber by adjusting the size of the aperture(s).
4) Do the final voicing by stringing the instrument and making fine adjustments to the aperture(s).

Note:
After each of the following steps, check the tuning to learn the result of the physical changes you have made. Make a copy of the worksheet in Appendix A to record the results of the adjustments you have made.

Step 1 - Tune the soundboard:
For mandolin construction, the soundboard should be glued to the rim (rib), and the instrument sanded to a ready-for-final-sanding state. Since guitar soundboards and backboards are typically glued to the rim in one operation, the boards must be tuned while attached to a support fixture, before gluing them to the rim.

Determine the initial tuning of the tone bars or braces as described on page 27, *Interpreting the tapped tone*.

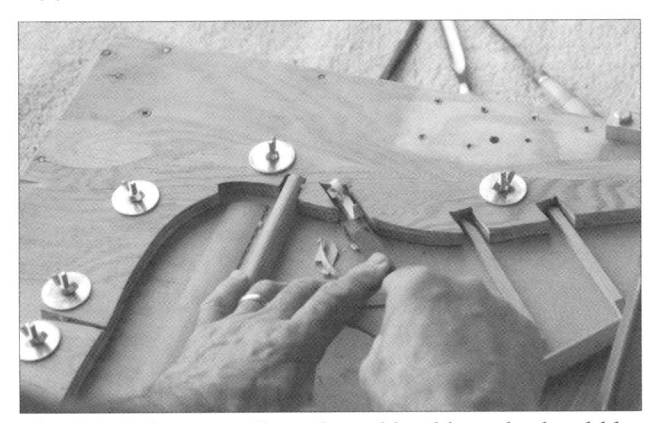

Fig. 5.1 Guitar soundboards and backboards should be clamped to a fixture for the tuning process.

Begin by tapering the ends of the tone bars first. This step will cause very little, if any, change in the tuning of the soundboard and will bring the bars to a rough-shaped state. (Removing wood from the center of the bars changes the tuning quickly.)

Changes in the tuning of the tone bars happen very slowly at first and may not be immediately evident until you have removed quite a bit of wood. You will arrive at a point in removing wood where the tone change becomes obvious, and you will begin to see major changes in frequency appear on the strobe tuner. Before trying to arrive at the final note, leave each tone bar 20 to 40 cents sharp bearing in mind that removing wood from the other tone bar will alter the pitch of the bar you have already tuned.

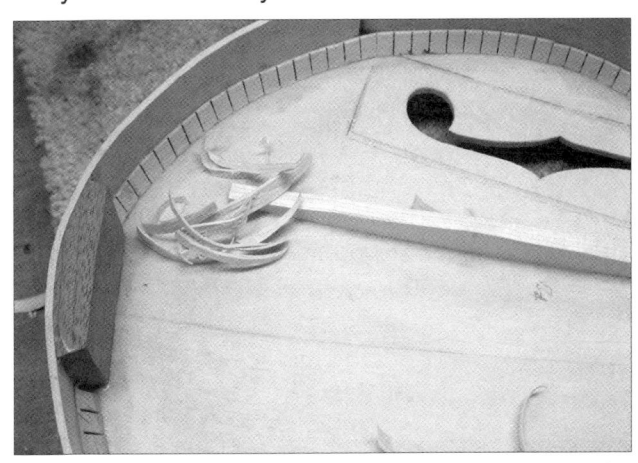

Fig. 5.2 Begin by shaving the ends of the bars to their almost-finished state as on this mandolin soundboard.

As soon as you get to the point of noticing a change in pitch, work carefully to remove only the wood you need to get each bar to a note that is a full-tone or semi-tone (i.e., no cents sharp or flat). Because tuning one bar affects the other bar, make small changes to each bar, alternating between bars. Do not try to tune one bar to its final target before proceeding to the next bar.

The objective is to arrive at notes that are zero cents sharp or flat. If you are tuning a bar and remove too much wood causing the bar to be flat,

29

The Art of Tap Tuning

you have two choices: 1) remove the bar and start over; or 2) reduce the tuning to the next lower half step.

If you shaved most, if not all, of the wood away from a bar and there was no change to the soundboard's tuning, it is an indication that the soundboard is entirely too thick. You should remove the bars completely, reduce the thickness of the soundboard, attach new bars, and repeat the tuning process.

Step 2 - Tune the backboard:
Determine the initial tuning of the backboard as described on page 27, *Interpreting the tapped tone*.

Arched-backboard instruments (e.g. guitars) typically have structural braces, and these can be tuned in much the same way as the bars on the soundboard. Carved backboard instruments (e.g. mandolins, violins) do not require bars because their shape gives them great strength in the absence of structural members. Carved backboards are tuned by removing wood from the backboard itself to lower the pitch.

As long as you use the same technique each time, you can tune the backboard in one of two ways:

1) The backboard should be clamped in a fixture and secured around its perimeter (Fig. 5.3). As a general rule, attaching it to a rim fixture enables a more audible and recognizable tone from the backboard compared to holding it free in the air. And, as described Chapter 3, a backboard will

Fig. 5.3 Held around its outer edges, this mandolin backboard is clamped to the support fixture for tuning. See Fig. 3.2 for a front view of the fixture.

Fig. 5.4 A sanding wheel on a hand drill is an easy (but messy) way to adjust the thickness of carved backboards while they are in the fixture. Periodically remove the backboard to check its thickness.

vibrate in different modes when secured around its perimeter than when held free in the air.

If the backboard is attached to a rim fixture as shown in Fig. 5.3, raise the fixture from the workbench or table, or position it vertically when you tap the backboard so that you do not invoke the resonant frequency of the air space under the fixture – you want to hear just the plate itself.

2) In the absence of making a fixture, a backboard can be tuned while held free in the air, pinched between two fingers (in the little stub where the neck attaches) and tapped in the center (Fig. 3.4). Remember the rule that a plate affixed to the rim will tune a fourth higher than the same plate held free in the air.

For a carved backboard, a sanding wheel on a hand drill is a great way to remove wood. This also helps to maintain the backboard's basic shape. Because the outside of the backboard is most likely in its near-final shape, focus on removing wood from the inside of the backboard.

Step 3 - Tune the air chamber:
Determine the initial tuning of the air chamber as described on page 27, *Interpreting the tapped tone*.

The soundboard and backboard should be attached to the rim and the entire instrument sanded to an almost-final sanding state.

As previously mentioned, each air chamber has an ideal aperture size that most ideally tunes that air chamber. Unfortunately, you can only find the

Chapter 5, Tuning and Voicing

Fig. 5.5 Regardless of the method you use to create the aperture, begin by cutting them undersize so they can be enlarged when tuning the air chamber.

ideal aperture size for your instrument by experimentation. Begin with apertures that are smaller than your intended design. To find the note, hold the instrument in the air as you tap on the center of the soundboard. The resonant frequency should be evident, but it may take you a few moments to find it on the tuner. Once you have determined the pitch of the air chamber and can demonstrate it repeatedly on the tuner, simply remove wood from the opening(s) until you arrive at the desired pitch. This step is very simple, but you must know what you are listening to (i.e., what the starting pitch is). As you make the aperture(s) larger, the pitch will increase. Obviously, you can't make the soundhole smaller unless you bind or build up the inside lip of the aperture(s).

Changing the size of a round soundhole requires removing wood from the entire circumference. Making small changes in the size of a round soundhole (e.g., acoustic guitar) will have a greater effect than small changes in the size of f-holes (e.g., mandolin) because you must remove wood from the entire inner edge of the soundhole to make it concentric. If you are tuning f-holes, you can widen them by removing wood from the sides of the openings, by making the two rounded ends larger, or a combination of both. Make small adjustments to both f-holes as you proceed.

For advanced luthiers, if you are seeking the optimum aperture for the size of your air chamber design, you need to devise a way to measure the change in amplitude. To do this, you will need to prepare a consistent means of tapping on the air chamber or otherwise exciting the soundboard and measuring the output with a decibelometer, a device that measures sound pressure (an inexpensive version is available at RadioShack). When you arrive at the optimum aperture size, the sound pressure will increase wildly (possibly 2 or 3 dB) and will then begin to decrease as the aperture gets too large. Even without a measuring device, it will be obvious to you when you are at the right point as the instrument you are tuning becomes entirely alive and highly sensitive to tapping. However, "if you go too far," it means that you have arrived at a point of no return and need to consider how to return to the optimal aperture (by adding binding or similar construction).

Step 4 - Voice the air chamber:
Final aperture adjustment is done at the end of the building process, before finishing, because it can most easily correct the many variables that contrib-

Fig. 5.6 To maintain the circular shape of a guitar soundhole, use a round sanding wheel and move it in a circular motion around the inside of the soundhole.

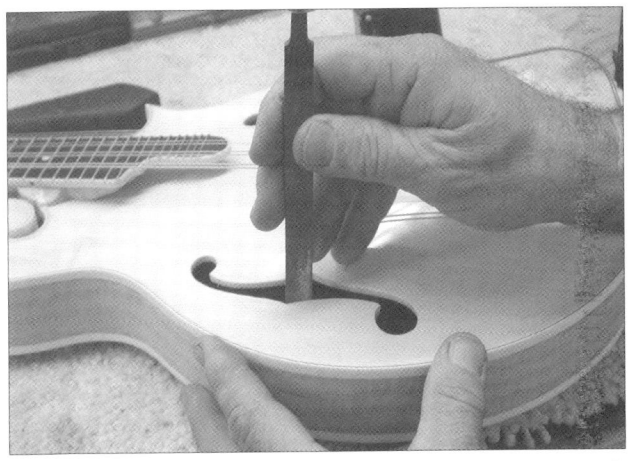

Fig. 5.7 For final voicing, the instrument is strung and the brought up to pitch. Final changes are made to the size of the aperture(s) with the soundboard fully loaded by the bridge.

The Art of Tap Tuning

ute to determining the resonant frequency of the air chamber. In addition, the instrument should be strung up to pitch so that the soundboard is loaded (which will slightly alter its previously tuned pitch). Now, you are ready to make final adjustments to the aperture(s) to "voice" the instrument.

With the strings tuned to pitch, place a felt or leather strip through the strings to damp their vibrations. To isolate the resonant frequency of the air chamber, lay the instrument on a padded surface to inhibit the backboard from vibrating. Tap near the crown of the soundboard close to the bridge, and measure the resonant frequency as you did in the tuning process. If everything in the construction process has worked properly, the strobe tuner should reveal that the air chamber is near your intended note. Unless you plan to bind the inside edge of the aperture to lower the pitch, all you can do at this point is remove wood to raise the pitch. Remove wood from the inner edge of the aperture and keep checking the tuner to measure the change. If you don't think you can arrive at your target note, try to tune the air chamber to the nearest full note (plus or minus zero cents).

Repeatability:
Use a copy of Appendix A to keep accurate notes of your adjustments. Once you have completed the tuning of the soundboard, backboard, and air chamber and have assembled the instrument, you will have a record of how the parts are tuned. This document will become an important reference for making your next instrument: repeating what you like or modifying what needs to be changed as you capture information and become more experienced. Thus, you know the ideal tunings for your next instrument as long as you use the same woods, similar plate thicknesses, bar locations, and final tunings. Repeatability and consistency are what you are striving for.

Notes:
1) Once you have completed an instrument, tuned the air chamber, and know the size of the aperture(s), you will be able to use that same <u>aperture</u> shape and size for future instruments that have an <u>air chamber</u> of the same size and shape.

2) Additional information about tuning a mandolin, specifics of the location of tone bars, and tuning the whole instrument is given in *The Ultimate Bluegrass Mandolin Construction Manual*, Hal Leonard Corporation, Milwaukee, WI.

3) For the banjo, head and air chamber tunings are described in *How to Set Up the Best Sounding Banjo*, Hal Leonard Corporation, Milwaukee, WI.

4) To facilitate the tuning process and isolate parts being tuned, braces and tone bars can be isolated by damping them with the finger or clamping a small rubber or leather caul to them. Small spring clamps, such as those available in office supply stores, work quite well to secure the caul in place.

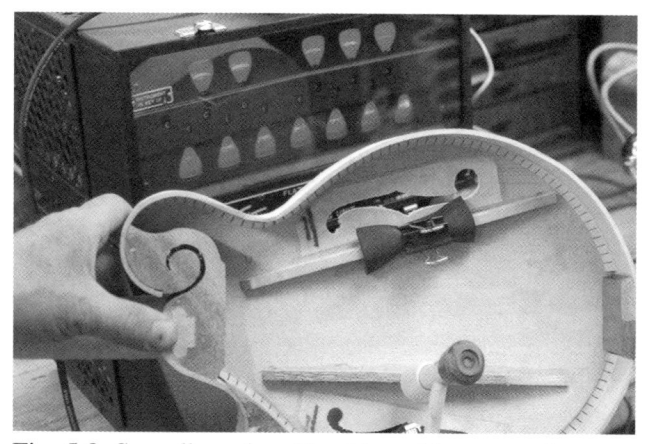

Fig. 5.8 Soundboard and backboard braces and tone bars can be isolated from those being tuned by clamping on a rubber caul to damp them.

... Suffice it to say that when making sound-boards of wood, which is very uneven in its standards, no two pieces ever being the same in texture, strength, and sensitiveness, better results will be secured if the vibration rate of various parts of the board and its resistance to a standard degree of pressure be taken as manufacturing standards rather than measurements of thickness or graduation.
<u>What Soundboards Do And How They Do It</u>, Lloyd Loar, Jacobs' Orchestra Monthly, October 1925

Chapter 6, Production Tuning

Deflection (structural) tuning:
In 1978, while trying to tune instruments in a noisy production environment where audible tap tuning was not practical, I developed a process that I call "deflection tuning." Deflection tuning assumes that if we measure how much a soundboard or backboard deflects under a specific load, we then know something about the inherent qualities of that backboard or soundboard. Specifically, we know its stiffness which, as you recall from earlier in this text, is a factor of tuning. It then follows that we can apply that same load to a new soundboard or backboard, remove wood until we arrive at the same deflection, which results in the boards being the same stiffness.

How do deflection tuning and tap tuning relate? Stiffness is a component of tuning, just as it is when you tune a string. For example, when a plain (unwound) .010″ string on a 26″ scale is tuned to a *D*, it exerts 13 pounds of tension. The corollary is if you begin in a slack state, put a tension gauge on that string and tension it to 13 pounds, it will produce a *D*. Thus, tension and pitch are inextricably connected components of tuning. When we tune a soundboard or backboard, we are adjusting its stiffness. So, we can first measure a tuned soundboard's stiffness by measuring its deflection under the strings' load, and then adjust the tone bars on another soundboard until we reach the desired deflection. The tuning results of both soundboards will be the same.

For soundboards and backboards, deflection measurements should be taken at four points, each equidistant from the center of the soundboard or backboard. If the boards are fitted with bars, the deflection measurements should be taken at points directly over the bars. Dial indicators are used to measure the deflection. The load delivered to the board being tuned should be the same as the load delivered to the board that was previously measured.

Example of deflection in adjustable bridge instruments:
Assume that a mandolin bridge exerts 38 pounds of down pressure on a soundboard when the strings are tuned to pitch (Fig. 2.1). Assume also that a properly tuned soundboard will sink or deflect .012″ at the bridge's centerline directly above the treble tone bar and .014″ at the bridge's centerline directly above the bass tone bar. Having determined this by measurement from another good-sounding soundboard, you could build a similarly-tuned soundboard by placing a 38 pound load on the soundboard (at the bridge centerline) and remove wood from the tone bars until the treble side sinks .012″ and the bass side sinks .014″. From a standpoint of stiffness, the newly tuned soundboard will be identical to the measured soundboard, even though their thickness measurements might be different. This is deflection tuning.

Fig. 6.1 As previously shown in Fig. 1.11, string load for movable bridges is measured in a fixture that simulates the same string scale and string break angle.

Example of deflection in fixed bridge instruments:
A fixture can also be constructed to test the loading of the soundboard on classical or acoustic steel string guitars. The distortion can be measured on

The Art of Tap Tuning

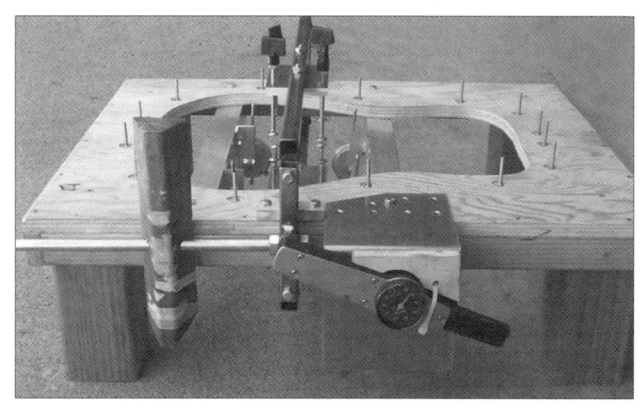

Fig. 6.2 This fixture simulates the torque or twisting load exerted on the soundboard by the strings of a fixed bridge instrument.

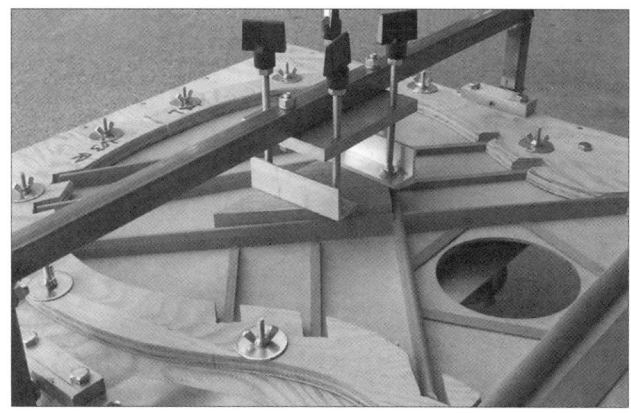

Fig. 6.3 The soundboard is clamped around its edges and the bridgeplate is locked to the swing arm.

Fig. 6.4 With a load applied to the swing arm, the deflection in front of and behind the bridge is measured by dial indicators below the fixture.

the soundboard of a guitar with its strings tuned to pitch. This information is then used to guide the process of shaving the braces on the new soundboard to make it deflect the same amount under a known load.

Comparing deflection and tap tuning:
The deflection process offers one unique advantage over the tap tuning method. In tap tuning, the stiffness of the tone bars and braces can be adjusted by tuning them to a note, but in so doing, we only learn about the global stiffness of the bar. In deflection tuning, we place several dial indicators along the structural lines of the soundboard and measure deflection at numerous points. The resultant tuning is localized and comprehensive, yielding not just tuned tone bars, but bars whose stiffness is adjusted along their entire length. The process might be overkill, but the idea certainly has merit, especially in cases where tone bars are lengthy such as those attached to piano soundboards.

Notes:
1) The deflection process can only be used after a sample soundboard and backboard have been successfully tap tuned. Deflection measurements are then taken of the tap tuned boards to measure their deflection under load, and these measurements are used to adjust future boards.

2) Although different species of woods will contribute different tonal qualities and result in soundboards and backboards that will produce different timbre, deflection tuning provides an excellent means for adjusting soundboards and backboards of the same species of woods to be identical to each other.

References:
If you would like to learn more about deflection tuning, an entire chapter is devoted to it (including some photos of various deflection tuning fixtures) in *The Luthier's Handbook*, Hal Leonard Corporation, Milwaukee, WI.

Appendix A, Tuning Record

brace 1	brace 2	brace 3	tone bar 1	tone bar 2	tone bar 3	bridgeplate	backboard	air chamber	comments

Permission granted to reproduce this page. *The Art of Tap Tuning*, Roger H. Siminoff, Hal Leonard Corporation, Milwaukee, WI.

The Art of Tap Tuning

Appendix B - Frequency Chart (A=440)

Appendix B
Frequency Chart (A=440)

	C	C#	D	D#	E	F	F#	G	G#	A	A#	B
Octave 1 Frequency	32.70	34.65	36.71	38.89	41.20	43.65	46.25	49.00	51.91	55.00	58.27	61.74
Octave 2 Frequency	65.41	69.30	73.42	77.78	82.41	87.31	92.50	98.00	103.83	110.00	116.54	123.47
Octave 3 Frequency	130.81	138.59	146.83	155.56	164.81	174.61	185.00	196.00	207.65	220.00	233.08	246.94
Octave 4 Frequency	261.62	277.18	293.66	311.13	329.63	349.23	369.99	392.00	415.30	440.00	466.16	493.88
Octave 5 Frequency	523.25	554.36	587.33	622.25	659.25	698.46	739.99	783.99	830.61	880.00	932.32	987.76
Octave 6 Frequency	1046.50	1108.73	1174.65	1244.50	1318.51	1396.91	1479.98	1567.98	1661.22	1760.00	1864.65	1975.52
Octave 7 Frequency	2092.99	2217.45	2349.31	2489.01	2637.01	2793.82	2959.95	3135.96	3322.44	3520.00	3729.30	3951.04

For a free Excel® version of this frequency chart that displays various frequencies for notes at user-definable settings of A= (i.e., A=431, A=445, etc.), please visit *www.siminoff.net*, [go to *Siminoff Banjo and Mandolin Parts*, and then to the *Downloads* page].

Permission granted to reproduce this page. *The Art of Tap Tuning*, Roger H. Siminoff, Hal Leonard Corporation, Milwaukee, WI.

Appendix C - Target Tunings

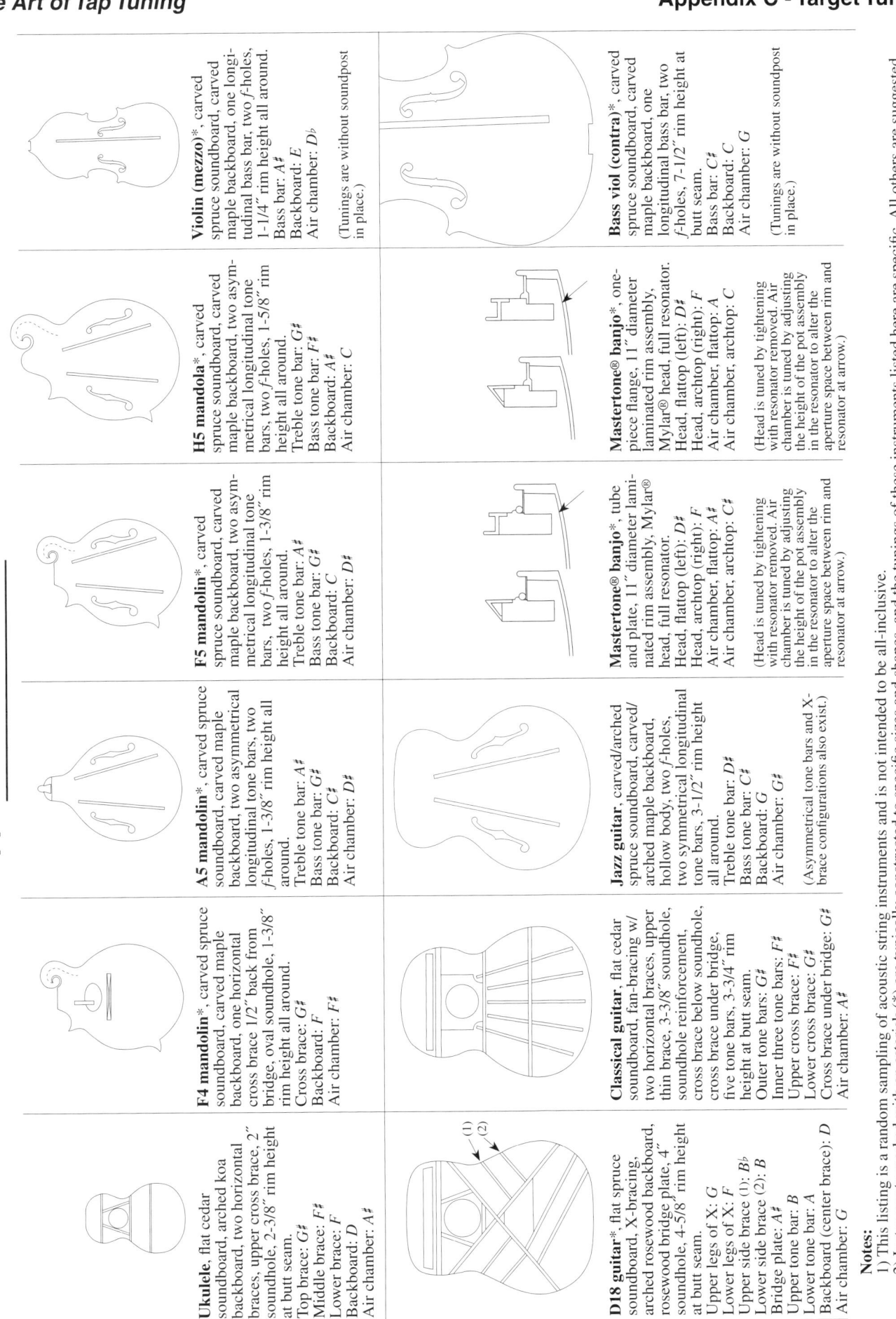

Ukulele, flat cedar soundboard, arched koa backboard, two horizontal braces, upper cross brace, 2" soundhole, 2-3/8" rim height at butt seam.
Top brace: $G\sharp$
Middle brace: $F\sharp$
Lower brace: F
Backboard: D
Air chamber: $A\sharp$

F4 mandolin*, carved spruce soundboard, carved maple backboard, one horizontal cross brace 1/2" back from bridge, oval soundhole, 1-3/8" rim height all around.
Cross brace: $G\sharp$
Backboard: F
Air chamber: $F\sharp$

A5 mandolin*, carved spruce soundboard, carved maple backboard, two asymmetrical longitudinal tone bars, two f-holes, 1-3/8" rim height all around.
Treble tone bar: $A\sharp$
Bass tone bar: $G\sharp$
Backboard: $C\sharp$
Air chamber: $D\sharp$

F5 mandolin*, carved spruce soundboard, carved maple backboard, two asymmetrical longitudinal tone bars, two f-holes, 1-3/8" rim height all around.
Treble tone bar: $A\sharp$
Bass tone bar: $G\sharp$
Backboard: C
Air chamber: $D\sharp$

H5 mandola*, carved spruce soundboard, carved maple backboard, two asymmetrical longitudinal tone bars, two f-holes, 1-5/8" rim height all around.
Treble tone bar: $G\sharp$
Bass tone bar: $F\sharp$
Backboard: $A\sharp$
Air chamber: C

Violin (mezzo)*, carved spruce soundboard, carved maple backboard, one longitudinal bass bar, two f-holes, 1-1/4" rim height all around.
Bass bar: $A\sharp$
Backboard: E
Air chamber: $D\flat$

(Tunings are without soundpost in place.)

D18 guitar*, flat spruce soundboard, X-bracing, arched rosewood backboard, rosewood bridge plate, 4" soundhole, 4-5/8" rim height at butt seam.
Upper legs of X: G
Lower legs of X: F
Upper side brace (1): $B\flat$
Lower side brace (2): B
Bridge plate: $A\sharp$
Upper tone bar: B
Lower tone bar: A
Backboard (center brace): D
Air chamber: G

Classical guitar, flat cedar soundboard, fan-bracing w/ two horizontal braces, upper thin brace, 3-3/8" soundhole, soundhole reinforcement, cross brace below soundhole, cross brace under bridge, five tone bars, 3-3/4" rim height at butt seam.
Outer tone bars: $G\sharp$
Inner three tone bars: $F\sharp$
Upper cross brace: $F\sharp$
Lower cross brace: $G\sharp$
Cross brace under bridge: $G\sharp$
Air chamber: $A\sharp$

Jazz guitar, carved/arched spruce soundboard, carved/arched maple backboard, hollow body, two f-holes, two symmetrical longitudinal tone bars, 3-1/2" rim height all around.
Treble tone bar: $D\sharp$
Bass tone bar: $C\sharp$
Backboard: G
Air chamber: $G\sharp$

(Asymmetrical tone bars and X-brace configurations also exist.)

Mastertone® banjo*, tube and plate, 11" diameter laminated rim assembly, Mylar® head, full resonator.
Head, flattop (left): $D\sharp$
Head, archtop (right): F
Air chamber, flattop: $A\sharp$
Air chamber, archtop: $C\sharp$

(Head is tuned by tightening with resonator removed. Air chamber is tuned by adjusting the height of the pot assembly in the resonator to alter the aperture space between rim and resonator at arrow.)

Mastertone® banjo*, one-piece flange, 11" diameter laminated rim assembly, Mylar® head, full resonator.
Head, flattop (left): $D\sharp$
Head, archtop (right): F
Air chamber, flattop: A
Air chamber, archtop: C

(Head is tuned by tightening with resonator removed. Air chamber is tuned by adjusting the height of the pot assembly in the resonator to alter the aperture space between rim and resonator at arrow.)

Bass viol (contra)*, carved spruce soundboard, carved maple backboard, one longitudinal bass bar, two f-holes, 7-1/2" rim height at butt seam.
Bass bar: $C\sharp$
Backboard: C
Air chamber: G

(Tunings are without soundpost in place.)

Notes:
1) This listing is a random sampling of acoustic string instruments and is not intended to be all-inclusive.
2) Instruments marked with an asterisk (*) are typically constructed to specific sizes and shapes, and the tunings of these instruments listed here are specific. All others are suggested.
3) Due to the wide range of body shapes, soundboard and backboard woods, aperture sizes, and bracing configurations, many tuning variations exist.
4) Generally speaking, instruments tuned to notes at concert pitch will be *bright* and *crisp*; instruments tuned a quarter tone off will be *warm* and *dark*. (See Appendix E.)
5) For more information on tuning banjos, see *How to Set Up the Best Sounding Banjo*, Hal Leonard Corporation, Milwaukee, WI.

Appendix D
A Brief History of Concert Pitch

Throughout musical history, "concert pitch" has not always been predicated on A, and A has not always been 440Hz. The earliest reference to specific tuning of A appears to be the Halberstadt organ (1361) that featured A tuned to 505.8Hz. In 1619, Praetorius (1571-1621) suggested a "suitable pitch" for A to be 424.2Hz. This pitch, sometimes called "mean pitch" agreed with Handel's (1685-1759) tuning fork (A422.5) in 1751 and the London Philharmonic's fork of A423.3 in 1820. This pitch prevailed for about two centuries during the periods of Handel, Haydn (1732-1809), Mozart (1756-1791), and Beethoven (1770-1827).

The first reference to the tuning of middle C at 260 was probably made by a contemporary of J.S. Bach (1685-1760), Joseph Sauveur (1654-1716), who is the first to have developed a method to precisely measure the exact pitch of a given note in cycles per second. He measured the pitches of organ pipes and vibrating strings, and defined the C of the musical scale at 256 cycles per second. (Today, we use the reference of Hertz, abbreviated as "Hz" to refer to vibrations or cycles per second.)

In the 1700s, 392Hz to 415Hz – commonly called "Baroque Pitch" – was used for Concert A.

In Germany, Mozart tuned to precisely C256. German instruments of the period 1780-1827 (and even replicas of those instruments) can only be tuned to A430.6 (the reference for the scale in which C256 occurs).

Early in the 19th Century, with the advent of military bands, an effort began to find a higher pitch to help the brass wind instruments sound "brighter."

The 1800s saw frequencies ranging from A420 to A425. (Early musicians called this "low pitch.") Czar Alexander of Russia called for a "brighter sound" at the Congress of Vienna in 1815, and so all crowned heads began to do the same. A commission with Hector Berlioz (1803-1869), Giacomo Meyerbeer (1791-1864), and Gioacchino Rossini (1792-1868) among its members was appointed by the French government. They prompted the passing of a law in 1859 establishing A at 435Hz.

This prompted Giuseppe Verdi to comment "we call A in Rome what is B-flat in Paris" and he attempted to raise the Italian standard to 432Hz (later to be invalidated at a conference in Austria in 1885 following protests by the British).

The well known German scientist, Hermann (Heinrich von) Helmholtz (1821-1894), referred to C as 256Hz in his work.

Despite protests from musicians that "Their Majesties" did not understand that new pitches often demanded the purchase of expensive instruments tuned to the new pitch, composers Liszt (1811-1886) and Richard Wagner (1813-1883) lobbied for the pitch to be raised. Wagner even had instruments made that could be played at A440 and above. By the mid-1800s, pitches were varying from A420 to A460 that resulted in total chaos for orchestral members.

By the end of the 1800s, the French government, with advice from Rossini, called for the "first standardization of the pitch of modern times." Later in the century, the pitch was raised to A430 and remained there well into the 20th Century (some called it "philosophical pitch" making a reference to the onslaught of scientific thought at the time).

In 1896, the Philharmonic Society adopted A439, and for some time this became the standard for the pianoforte trade.

In the early 1920s, the development of broadcasting fueled a growing interest in finding international agreement on concert pitch. Measurements performed by the Physikalische Technische Bundesanstalt confirmed that the world's orchestras of that period were using a wide array of "standard pitches" for A. England was A443.5, Czechoslovakia was A443, Denmark was A439.5, and Holland was A439.9.

Then, in 1939, an international conference held in London and attended by representatives from Germany, Great Britain, Holland, and Italy (with Switzerland and the United States voting via absentee memorandum) unanimously adopted "A440 as the standard pitch for the treble clef."

Appendix D - A Brief History of Concert Pitch

Despite the agreement of *A*440 as standard pitch, the French, the New York Metropolitan Orchestra, and many other prominent orchestras around the world continued to tune *A* between 432Hz and 435Hz until the beginning of World War II.

Well into the early 1900s, all Western textbooks on physics, sound, acoustics, and music referred to the physical pitch or scientific pitch as *C*256Hz (in which *A*=430.6Hz).

In 1953, at a meeting of the International Standardizing Organization (ISO) in London, there was an effort to once and for all establish *A* at 440Hz. The suggestion was passed by the members, but ignored by a significant number of notable musicians and music organizations (who were not invited). The French accused the British instrument makers of catering to the U.S. jazz trade (which tuned to *A*440), complaining that classical orchestras would be dependant on what "jazz players were dictating." A subsequent referendum among thousands of French musicians voted overwhelmingly to remain at *A*432Hz.

The most recent attempt to standardize pitch was in 1971 when the European Economic Community (EEC) passed a "recommendation" to fix international pitch at *A*440Hz – but not every country or organization has accepted the recommendation.

On the extreme side, Highland bagpipers are currently using a pitch that ranges between *A*476 and *A*480 with an effort to get a "brighter" sound (the perception being that higher pitch means brighter sound). Indian Shruti players use *A*444, and French flautists use *A*442.

So, today (2007), there really is no global agreement on "concert pitch," and everyone is still very much on their own depending on where they play their music.

Note:
Currently, the medical profession uses *C*128 and *C*256 tuning forks to test neurological response. While these forks are readily available to the medical community, they serve little purpose for musicians because: a) the forks are not as precisely tuned as musical forks; and b) they are not tuned to today's concert pitch of *A*440.

Appendix E
What Was Loar Hearing?

Lloyd Allayre Loar (1886-1943) was a performing musician, composer, acoustical engineer, and musical instrument designer who made numerous major contributions to the world of music. He worked for the Gibson Mandolin-Guitar Company (Kalamazoo, MI) from 1920-1925 in the role of acoustical engineer. During his tenure at Gibson, he introduced the process of "tap tuning" to ensure that all parts of the instrument contributed to the whole of the sound. After leaving Gibson, Loar founded the ViviTone Company and, later, the Acousti-Lectric Company (both in Kalamazoo, MI). Loar received 11 U.S. patents. For more information about Loar, visit *www.siminoff.net*.

What was Loar hearing?
A poem entitled "Miniver Cheevy" by Edwin Arlington Robinson talks about a dreamer who always thought about what was and what could be. And, for others of us, we often think about times past, and compare what is now to what might have been. So, while we marvel at the magical sound of Loar-signed F5 mandolins, one might stop and think, "What was Loar hearing when he was building and playing these instruments? Did he hear the rich throaty sound that we admire in an F5 today? Or did he hear something else?"

Gibson's labels of the "Master Model" instruments that bore Loar's signature attest – and we've proven – that "The top, back, tone-bars, and air-chamber of this instrument were tested, tuned ..."

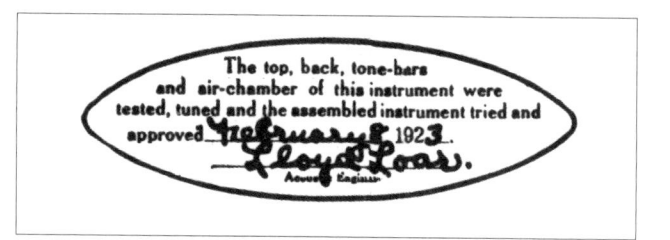

Fig. E.1 This facsimile of the original signature label used in the Gibson Master Model series instruments appeared in the 1924 F5 mandolin brochure.

We know the instruments of Loar's day were new, not broken in, and absent of 80 years of aging characteristics we attribute to older instruments. We know the strings were a different composition than those we use today. We know that the plectrums of the period were made of a different type of plastic than we use today.

But there is something else that makes the original F5s unique, and it relates to precisely how they were tuned.

Tunings in the early 20th Century
In the 1920s, when Lloyd Loar was at Gibson designing instruments, he focused on tuning the various parts of the instrument to specific notes that were part of concert pitch. This "tuning" (or "tap tuning") is the art of building an instrument so that each of its tone-producing parts resonate in harmony with the notes being played on the strings. In this regard, the components of the instrument's body support, amplify, resonate with, and augment the frequencies being sent to the soundboard by the strings. This is what gives an instrument its "tone color" or "timbre."

Loar specified that the backboard of the F5 mandolins were to be tuned to *C*128, the treble tone bar to *A#*228, the bass bar to *A♭*203, and the air chamber to *D#*152.

Note:
"*C*128" represents a *C* note whose frequency is 128 cycles per second, more properly stated as 128Hz. *A#*228 represents an *A* sharp note whose frequency is 228 cycles per second or 228Hz. *Ab*203 represents an *A* flat whose frequency is 203 cycles per second or 203Hz, and *D*152 represents a *D* whose frequency is 152 cycles per second or 152Hz.

The idea of tuning each of the parts of the instrument wasn't fantasy or Gibson marketing hype. It is something the company really did during Loar's tenure from 1920 to 1925 (and then later, for a period of about a year with the introduction of the F5L in 1978). The process was time consuming and exacting, and one can only surmise that this led Gibson to discontinue the tuning process when Loar left the company in 1925.

While the art of tap tuning pre-dated Loar by several hundred years, the introduction of tap tuning to fretted instruments was clearly one of Loar's major contributions to both Gibson and to the world of fretted acoustic string instruments.

Does tap tuning work?
The results can be scientifically proven, and those of you who have followed my work know that I

Appendix E - *What Was Loar Hearing?*

have performed tuning tests many times in many different ways. One simple experiment is to hang an F5 on an instrument stand and place a speaker on another stand facing, and close to, the mandolin. Then, subject the mandolin to a range of frequencies, via the speaker, from a sweep frequency oscillator (a device that produces a range of pure tones). As the various parts of the mandolin vibrate in sympathy with the tones from the speaker, they vibrate more responsively when their resonant frequency is attained. For example, if the air chamber is tuned to a *D♯*, the mandolin howls when the speaker produces a *D♯*. The responses can be measured by using a decibelometer and watching for the highest reading as you sweep through the frequencies. To determine the precise frequency of that loudest point, use a frequency counter and simply read the results on its panel.

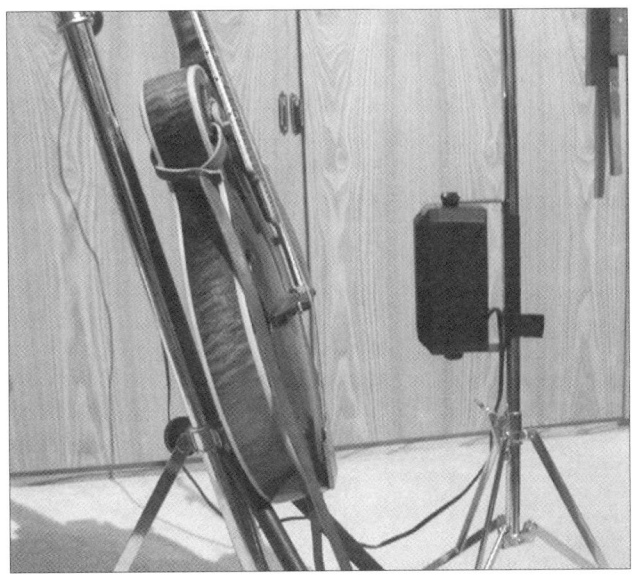

Fig. E.2 To test the premise, this original Loar-signed F5 was positioned in front of a speaker that was connected to the sweep frequency oscillator in Fig. E.3.

Note:
A decibelometer is a device that measures sound pressure and provides a numerical value of the relative loudness of sound.

The next step is to determine which part is vibrating. In these tests, you can literally feel the backboard pulsing wildly as it vibrates in sympathy with the frequency oscillator. And you can feel the treble and bass tone bars individually vibrating in sympathy to their tuned notes merely by putting your fingers lightly on the soundboard. And, the air chamber howls as you arrive at its resonant frequency. These tests are very simple to perform, and the results are quite dramatic.

Fig. E.3 The speaker is driven by a sweep-frequency oscillator that is connected to a measuring device to report the precise frequency. Here it indicates 128Hz.

Variations of this test can be performed by placing fabric in one or both of the *f*-holes to modify the air chamber's tuning, attaching a special weighted clamp to one or both of the tone bars to dampen them, or using some method to isolate one component of the structure. These variations test how each component alters the way the instrument responds. The results of the tests clearly point to the fact that changing the tuning of the tone bars has a direct affect on the overall tonal characteristics of the instrument.

What did Loar do?
Loar saw to it that the instruments under his watch were carefully tuned. And, the results speak for themselves. Tuning works, and Loar-signed instruments really do sound great.

But, let's not forget the question: What was Loar hearing?

It wasn't what we hear today!

Clearly, the instruments under his care were precisely tuned. But Loar didn't hear what we hear because in 1925 Loar was using *C*256 as the center point for his concert pitch. The scale that uses *C*256 is predicated on fourth octave *A* being 430.6Hz.

Today, our concert pitch is *A*440 (not *A*430.6).

When we play an original Loar-signed "tuned" F5 today, our strings are tuned to concert pitch which is predicated on *A*440, but the parts of the instrument are tuned to the concert pitch of Loar's time – *C256* – in which *A* is *A430.6*. Basically, a quarter step or quarter tone lower. The difference in frequencies is just outside the threshold of unpleasant "beats." This chart compares the relative notes of the two tunings:

Concert pitch:	A440	C256*
Backboard	C131	C128
Treble tone bar	A#233	A#228
Bass tone bar	G#208	G#203
Air chamber	D#155	D#152

*Pitch used by Lloyd Loar in 1925 to tune F5 mandolins.

Fig. E.4 The difference in pitch of the parts of the F5 mandolin tuned to concert pitch of *A440* compared to concert pitch of *C256* (in which *A*=430.6).

As a result, the soundboard, backboard, and air chamber of a Loar-signed F5 are tuned a quarter tone lower than our concert pitch of today. But, interestingly, this difference seems to add a pleasant "coloring" to the tone of the original F5s which, aside from being made 80 years ago, is one of the main attributes – if not THE main attribute – that sets their timbre apart from other mandolins. It is much like what experienced piano tuners do when they adjust one of the two or three strings of a particular note so that it is not quite in unison. Piano tuners call this "finessing," and it provides a unique warmth not achievable when tuning two or three strings of a given note in perfect unison.

Tuning new F5s to sound like Loar-signed F5s
Philosophically and scientifically, it is optimum to tune the various parts of an instrument to notes that are part of the scale to which the strings are tuned. And, since instruments that are played in the United States today are typically tuned using *A440* as the reference, then it holds that *A440* should be the reference for tuning the instrument's parts.

However, in order to build a new instrument that delivers the timbre of an aged Loar-signed F5 mandolin (or L5 guitar, or H5 mandola), the parts of the instrument should be tuned to notes that use *C256* as reference.

To be successful in this attempt, you should:

1) Believe in the premise of tap tuning.

2) Use a strobe tuner or software tuner that will enable you to modify the concert pitch to some note other than *A440* (See Note 2 below).

3) Tune the instrument's parts to the notes where *C*=256 (see Fig. E.4).

4) Break in the instrument with hours of continuous playing.

Notes:
1) You can download a free musical frequency calculator (Excel® spreadsheet) from *www.siminoff.net* from the "Downloads" page (in the "Banjo and Mandolin Parts" section). This will enable you to set the fourth octave *A* to any frequency and read the frequencies for all the notes of the eight contemporary octaves.

2) Some tuners, such as the Peterson Model 490 or Model 590 strobe tuner, can be set to *A430* (or any other frequency for *A*).

Appendix F
More on Soundboards

In the early 1920s, The Gibson Mandolin-Guitar Company (as it was known then) made bold steps in the development of acoustic string instruments under the leadership of Lloyd A. Loar. It was during this time that the company promoted its "Master Model" line that featured mandolins, mandolas, and guitars that were tap tuned. Today, these instruments are heralded as best-of-class by musicians worldwide.

Loar was a highly-motivated individual whose achievements included musician, composer, musical engineer, instrument designer, entrepreneur, and author. For a brief period, Loar wrote a column entitled "Acoustics for the Musician" for the *Jacobs' Orchestra Monthly*, a prominent music industry magazine of the time. It seems fitting to include this article that appeared in the October 1925 issue.

What Sound Boards Do And How They Do It

Acoustics for the Musician
No. 7, Continued
By Lloyd Loar, Mus. M.

Tone-bars or bass-bars on the underside of sound-boards are to assist the board to vibrate as a unit, instead of in sections as the board would do if left to its own devices, and as the disks used in scientific work do vibrate. These bars must have sufficient rigidity to carry the fundamental string vibration instantly to each end of the board; and must be light enough in weight not to handicap the bridge in moving the top, and they must be elastic enough to permit the top to include in its complete vibration the shorter and more rapid vibrations which represent the overtone string vibrations and produce the overtone patterns in the sound wave. Without bars of this sort the sound-board must be much smaller so it will vibrate as a unit, and the tone is consequently less than it could be. The larger the sound-board area possible to vibrate simultaneously, the bigger the tone possible to the instrument, and well-planned tone bars make it possible to use a longer sound-board and consequently to construct instruments that produce more tone. A comparison of the sound-board of the conventional mandolin–which has its greatest length from the edge of the round sound hole next the bridge to the tailpiece, and is totally innocent of tone bars–with the sound-board of a violin, goes far to explain their difference in tonal power.

It is true that the sound-board of a mandolin of the above type has braces to give it strength to resist the string pressure and to keep it from caving in back of the sound-hole, but these braces are not tone bars. Tone bars are not to make the top stronger, but to make it possible to vibrate a larger board as a unit. A violin top is quite adequate in strength to support the string pressure without either bass-bar or sound-post, but without them it would not vibrate violently and completely enough to give good violin tone.

In order to appreciate how the sound-board reproduces the overtone vibrations and puts them in their proper place and proportion in the sound wave, we must remember how these overtone vibrations are generated by the string and communicated through the bridge to the top. As the string makes a complete vibration it depresses and releases the sound-board, which makes a complete vibration, down from the string and up toward the string. During this complete string vibration, numerous other vibration waves started previously and representing the over-tones are still affecting the string, each one giving the bridge a quick push in its turn between the beginning and finish of the complete vibration. Consequently, the bridge gives the board an exactly timed series of little impulses while the board is making each of its complete vibrations. These smaller impulses are always weaker than the fundamental or main vibrations and they do not extend as far from the bridge as the fundamental vibrations; in fact, the more of them that are included in the fundamental, and the more rapidly they occur, the smaller the area of sound-board around the bridge that they affect.

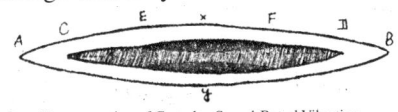

Representation of Complex Sound-Board Vibration

The drawing herewith may assist rather feebly in giving an idea of how this complex sound-board vibration would look if we could see it. This is not to be considered as anywhere near an exact representation. It is extremely allegorical, so to speak.

This article has been transcribed verbatim with no editorial corrections or modifications.

We are to imagine the bridge as being near the center of the board. A-B is the board lengthwise and vibrating in response to the fundamental string vibration; C-D is the vibration in response to the first overtone vibration; and E-F, in response to the second overtone vibration. From X to Y is only one-half of the board's complete vibration, from X to Y and return to X is a complete vibration of A-B. So, during one A-B vibration, we have two C-D vibrations and four E-F vibrations.

The outside edges of C-D and E-F are in effect, nodal points, but they are not found at any certain place on the board; as the tone changes in color or power the nodal lines shift, even though the pitch of the tone remains the same. A well constructed sound-board–such as that of one of the best Stradivarius violins–is planned to encourage these partial vibrations which give the tone its color. In the center the board is thickest; a short distance from the center it is slightly thinner, forming an irregularly shaped plane around the center; around this plane is another still thinner, and so to the outside edge of the board which is thinnest of all. In an instrument like the violin the board becomes thicker at its outside edge, but for mechanical reasons only, so that where it is glued to the rim there will be enough material to give the body the necessary mechanical strength.

I am again reduced to the necessity of illustrating more fully with a sketch, one that gives more exactly an idea of these diminishing thicknesses of sound-boards, known as graduations, but not to be taken as an exact representation of any sound-board, so far as actual efficient graduation is concerned. It's merely to give an idea of how these graduations should be planned.

Cross-Section of Graduated Sound-Board

This sketch shows a cross section lengthwise at the center along the line A-B in our second sketch. The second sketch shows our same board from the underside with the different thicknesses indicated by the different shadings, the darkest indicating the greatest thickness of the board, and the shading being less heavy as the board becomes thinner.

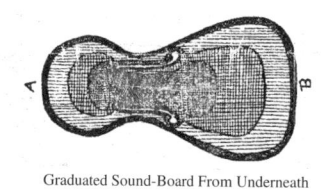

Graduated Sound-Board From Underneath

In a finished board, these different thicknesses shade into each other very gradually, being discernible only with a pair of callipers.

It will be remembered I mentioned that the nodes of vibration on the board shift their position even though the pitch of the tone sounded doesn't change. Obviously, the lines of demarcation, as shown in our second sketch, will seldom correspond to the actual nodes formed as the board vibrates. The board is planned so that it accommodates the average vibration rate (pitch and tone color) of the instrument; then the sound-holes, air chamber, and back are planned so they lend themselves more fully to vibration to which the top is not so friendly. Then the gradual diminishing in thickness of the top, instead of being a series of abrupt steps as shown in the sketch, shade into each other imperceptibly and make it easier for the top to accommodate these shifts in the nodal lines of the board. Consequently, the completed instrument can have, if made correctly, a well-balanced scale from its lowest to its highest note; that is, no one note will be stronger than any other note, and neither will there be any sudden uncontrollable changes in tone color as the scale progresses from note to note.

Sound-holes serve a dual purpose; they tune the air-chamber to the most desirable pitch and allow the air in the air chamber to contact with the outside air and thus put its vibration pattern in the sound-wave, and they make the top more sensitive without making it very much less sturdy. That is, if sound-holes are proportioned and placed right, the sound-board gains in sensitiveness a great deal more than it loses in strength. We'll consider sound-holes separately in our next instalment, so detailed explanation of how they do this necessary thing will be reserved for then.

Efficient Sound-Board Characteristics

Summing up briefly, sound-boards should be light in weight, yet of considerable strength and elasticity. Being made of material that has its own natural vibration rate, boards should be planned so they retain the characteristics that give them this vibration rate, be as nearly equal in response as possible to all vibration rates, no matter how complex. They must be planned so they vibrate as a unit, and so their sectional vibrations are contained in and a part of their complete vibration, instead of being independent of it. Yet a well-built sound-board does all these things faithfully as long as it has life and vitality.

It is not practicable to give here detailed directions as to how this can be done, yet plenty of space and time would permit of such directions. Suffice it to say that when making sound-boards of wood, which is very uneven in its standards, no two pieces ever being the same in texture, strength, and sensitiveness, better results will be secured if the vibration rate of various parts of the board and its resistance to a standard degree of pressure be taken as manufacturing standards rather than measurements of thickness or graduation.

An arched sound-board is always better than a flat one. The arched construction gives greater strength for its weight than flat construction. Flat boards need to be reinforced by braces which interfere with the necessary vibration patterns. It is of no help to decrease the string pressure so that a flat top can be used without braces. With 27 pounds total string pressure, as in our experimental violin, the force exerted by any one note from the strings is not great, and the small impulses from the numerous overtone impulses are extremely delicate. If the string pressure is reduced, some of the overtone impulses have insufficient strength to vibrate even a flat top and so are completely lost.

It must be remembered that these various factors do not change in exact proportion to each other. That is, if we reduce the string pressure half, we can't reduce the sound-board resistance half and get the same result. This is true throughout the whole instrument and it's also true of all instruments.

Then it's not only true that the board vibrates more violently and rapidly at its center under the bridge and so should be thicker there for that reason, because being thicker, it has a higher vibration rate, but it is also true that as the whole board has to be vibrated from its center under the bridge, the thickest part of the board should be in the center. It is easier for the heavy part of the board to move the light part, than vice versa.

As the impulses from the bridge travel through the top, they lose force as they travel; with a board thick at the center and becoming thinner towards its edges, these impulses find less weight to move as they grow weaker, and so the strongest of them are carried clear to the edge of the board.

A flat board does not lend itself to this tapering from thick to thin construction, while an arched board does. In fact, there are no arguments in favor of a flat sounding board except that it's cheaper and easier to manufacture.

BANJO SOUND-BOARDS

Just a word to banjoists. The elasticity of the banjo sound-board (or head) is secured artificially by tightening the head, consequently it can be controlled very easily. This gives the banjo player a considerable advantage if he cares to avail himself of it. By a little experimenting, he can determine the pitch or tone of the head at which his banjo sounds best, identify this pitch by tapping it lightly with the fleshy part of the thumb or finger while the strings are muffled, and then keep the head tuned to that pitch.

It will be remembered in our article on string instrument bridges in the April and June issues of JACOBS' ORCHESTRA MONTHLY, mention was made of the fact that more vibration was communicated from the strings through the bass side of the bridge than through the treble. To assist in doing this, sound-boards are made slightly stiffer and less sensitive on the bass side than on the treble side. Because of this previous comment, detailed explanation of the graduation in sound-boards most favorable to this, is not mentioned here. This extra stiffness can be secured in many ways: by tone bars so planned, by the board being slightly thicker on that side, by a sound-post, as in the violin family, or by all three of them or any two of them. Our next instalment will discuss this more fully as it deals with sound-holes, tone bars, sound-posts, etc.

The banjoist, to give his banjo this advantage should, after the head is tuned to what he has decided is the best pitch, tighten slightly the four opposing brackets (two at each end) between which the treble foot of his bridge rests. The improvement in his banjo tone may not be startling, but in most cases (depending on the texture of the head) it will be noticeable to a keen ear, and–every little helps.

Lest these conclusions regarding sound-boards seem too much like guesses, a short summary of how they were arrived at may be desirable. Vibrating boards of various instruments were tested over their entire surface with tuning forks, with a long sound-post of spruce held between the board and a sensitive tooth or the tip of the tongue, with brass reeds tuned to various overtones in the tone sounded, and glued to the board in such a way that when the part of the board to which they were glued vibrated at that pitch the reed responded, and with small diaphragms tuned to various pitches and connected to various parts of the top by a long rod. Slowly vibrating tops were also examined under a powerful microscope.

Consequently, I feel safe in assuming that the theories advanced herein are more than guesses and that they have considerable basis in fact.

Appendix G
Recommended Reading

The Acoustical Foundations of Music (2nd edition), John Backus, New York, W. W. Norton & Company, 1977.

Collected Papers on Acoustics, Wallace Clement Sabine, New York, Dover Publications, 1964.

The Effects of Noise on Man (2nd edition), Karl D. Kryter, St. Louis, Academic Press, 1985.

Experiments in Tone Perception, R. Plomp, Soesterberg, Netherlands, Institute for Perception, 1966.

Fundamentals of Musical Acoustics (2nd, revised edition), Arthur H. Benade, New York, Dover Publications, 1990.

A Guide to Musical Acoustics (republication of 1956 edition), Harry Lowery, New York, Dover Publications, 1966.

Handbook of Noise Measurement (6th edition), Arnold P. G. Peterson and Ervin E. Gross, Jr., West Concord, MA, General Radio, 1967.

How to Setup the Best Sounding Banjo, Roger H. Siminoff, Milwaukee, WI, Hal Leonard Corporation, 1999.

The Luthier's Handbook, Roger H. Siminoff, Milwaukee, WI, Hal Leonard Corporation, 2002.

Music and Sound, L. S. Lloyd, Westport, CT, Greenwood Press (Ayer Co. Pub.), 1937.

Music, Physics and Engineering (2nd edition), Harry F. Olson, New York, Dover Publications, 1967.

Music, Sound, and Sensation, Fritz Winckel, New York, Dover Publications, 1967.

Musical Acoustics (4th edition), Charles A. Culver, New York, McGraw-Hill Book Company, 1956.

Musical Acoustics: An Introduction, Donald E. Hall, Belmont, California, Wadsworth Publishing Company, 1980.

On the Sensations of Tone, Hermann Helmholtz, New York, Dover Publications, 1954.

Physics and the Sound of Music (2nd edition), John S. Rigden, New York, John Wiley & Sons, 1985.

Alexander Wood's the Physics of Music (7th edition reprint), Alexander Wood and J. M. Bowsher, Westport, CT, Greenwood Press, 1981.

Piano Tuning, J. Cree Fischer, New York, Dover Publications, 1975 (free download available through the Project Gutenberg – www.gutenberg.org).

Science & Music, Sir James Jeans, New York, Dover Publications, Inc., 1968.

The Science of Sound (3rd edition), Thomas D. Rossing, F. Richard Moore, and Paul A. Wheeler, Reading, MA, Addison-Wesley Publishing Company, 2001.

Sound and Music (2nd edition), Rev. J. A. Zahm, Chicago, A. C. McClurg & Co., 1900.

The Theory of Sound (vol. 2), John William Strutt and Baron Rayleigh, New York, Dover Publications, 1945.

The Ultimate Bluegrass Mandolin Construction Manual, Roger H. Siminoff, Milwaukee, WI, Hal Leonard Corporation, 2004.

References

Helmholtz, Hermann, 1954, *On the Sensations of Tone,* New York, Dover Publications, Inc.

Loar, Lloyd, 1925, *What Soundboards Do And How They Do It,* Chicago, Jacobs' Orchestra Monthly.

Norris, John, Peterson ElectroMusical, Alsip, IL, (personal communication).

Rigden, John. S., 1977, *Physics and the Sound of Music,* New York, John Wiley & Sons.

Rossing, Thomas, D., 1982, *The Science of Sound,* Reading, MA, Addison-Wesley Publishing Company.

Strutt, John William and Rayleigh, Baron, 1945, *The Theory of Sound,* New York, Dover Publications.

Wood, Alexander, 1944, *The Physics of Music,* London, Chapman and Hall.

Zahm, J. A, 1900, *Sound and Music,* Chicago, A. C. McClurg & Co.

Index

Acousti-Lectric Company, 40
air chamber, 15
air chamber size, 19
amplitude, 1, 3
anisotropic (attributes):
    maple, 2
    spruce, 2
apertures, 4, 13, 19
attack
    duration of, 5
    location of, 5
    method of, 5
Bach, J.S., 38
backboard
    resonant frequency, 13
    tuning, 30
banjo soundboards, 37, 45
beats, 12, 14
Beethoven, 38
Behringer compressor, 26
bowing (to emit tone), 12, 16
brace(s), 9, 17
    location, 21, 22
    tuning, 22, 29
bracing
    "X" bracing, 21, 22
    asymmetrical bracing, 21
    fan bracing, 21, 22
    symmetrical bracing, 21
bridgeplates, 17, 22
bridge
    energy transfer, 7, 8
    fixed bridge, 7, 33
    location of, 6, 10
    movable bridge, 7, 34
    violin bridge, 8
cents, 20, 36
compression, 1, 2, 13
compressors
    Behringer, 26
    Ibanez, 26
    Marshall, 26
concert pitch, 11, 16, 38
Congress of Vienna, 38
Conn, C.G., 26
coupled system, 12, 18
cycles per second, 3
damped, damping, 2, 3
decibelometer, 31
decibels, 1
deflection tuning, 24, 33
down pressure, 8, 8
duration of attack, 5
effective power (from body), 13
f-holes, 4, 12, 19
F5 mandolin, 16, 40

finish, affects on tuning, 23
fixed bridges, 7, 33
frequency, 3, 36
frequency oscillator, 41
fundamental, 4, 5
Gibson Company, 40
Gibson Mandolin-Guitar Company, 11, 43
graduated soundboard, 44
Guild, 22
Halberstadt organ, 38
hammers, tap tune, 24, 25
Handel, 38
Haydn, 38
Helmholtz, Hermann, 15, 38
Hertz, 3, 38
Baroque Pitch, 38
Highland bagpipers, 39
Hz, 3
Ibanez compressor, 26, 28
International Standards Organization, 39
ISO, 39
Jacobs' Orchestra Monthly, 33, 43
lateral vibrations, 6, 10
load (from bridge), 15
loading, soundboard, 8, 16
Loar, Lloyd, 11, 16, 21, 33, 40, 43
location of attack, 5
location of the bar, 18
London Philharmonic, 38
longitudinal vibrations, 6
loudness, 1
Marshall compressor, 26
Martin, C.F., 21
mass, 20
method of attack, 5
Meyerbeer, Giacomo, 38
Mossman, 22
movable bridges, 7, 24
Mozart, 38
oval soundhole, 21
Ovation, 22
partials, 5
Peterson ElectroMusical, 26, 27
plates, 17
quarter tone, 11, 37
rarefaction, 1, 2, 13
Rayleigh, Lord Baron, 29
reference tuning, 23
resonant frequency, 15, 20, 22
restoring force, 9
Rigden, John, 12
Rossing, Thomas D., 17
Rossini, Gioacchino, 38
scalloped braces, 18
shape of the bar, 18
sound pressure, 1

soundboard
    deflection, 16
    graduation, 10, 44
    loading, 8, 15, 16
    resonant frequency, 13
    stiffness, 10
    thickness, 10
    tuning, 29
stiffness (soundboard, backboard), 10
string break angle, 8, 15
strobe tuners, 25, 42
StroboSoft™, 27, 28
sustain, 9
Tacoma Narrows Bridge, 14
tap tune hammer, 24, 25
tap tuning reference note, 11
target tunings, 22, 37
test instrument, 23
threshold of hearing, 3
timbre, 1
tone bar
    to adjust stiffness, 9
    to adjust tone, 4
    location, 21
    removing wood from, 17, 29
    tuning, 22
transmission of vibrations
    through maple, 2
    through spruce, 2
tuning
    air chamber, 13, 15, 19, 24, 30
    backboard, 18, 24, 30
    bowing 24
    deflection, 24
    fixture, 18, 30
    hammers, 24, 25
    ideal note, 14, 37
    methods, 24
    quarter tone off, 11
    record, 35
    soundboard, 18, 24, 29
    to concert pitch 11
    voicing, 29
    where to tap, 17
tuning fork, 3, 21
tympanic membrane, 1
Verdi, Giuseppe, 38
vibration of musical strings, 4
vibrations, lateral, 6, 10
vibrations, longitudinal, 6
violin f-holes, 19
ViviTone Company, 40
voicing the air chamber, 29, 31
Wagner, Richard, 38
wolf note, 14
Zahm, J.A., 1

About the Author

Roger H. Siminoff, one of the foremost authorities on musical acoustics, has been designing, building, researching, playing, and writing about acoustic musical instruments and their makers for the past 45 years.

Born in Newark, New Jersey, Siminoff's music appreciation developed at age 10 when he began to play the piano, but found he was more intrigued by what was happening inside the piano than outside of it. Siminoff first built a pedal steel guitar when he was 18. The steel guitar was soon followed by the construction of a five-string banjo, planting the seed for a life-long dedication to musical acoustics and the art of luthiery.

In the early 1970s, Siminoff expanded his interest to making mandolin parts, and he designed and built unique carving machines to shape the precise contours of instrument necks and the delicate graduations of mandolin top and back plates.

His affiliation with Ray Donnelley of Cedar Knolls Acoustical Labs (NJ) gave him greater insight into the acoustical properties of resonant bodies and plates, and he began to build acoustical models to test the tonal properties of woods, braces, air chambers, and apertures.

In 1974, Siminoff founded *Pickin' Magazine* and that publication was followed by the launch of *Frets Magazine* in 1978. For these publications, Siminoff did extensive research on musical acoustics, conducted numerous interviews, and wrote countless articles on the subject.

In the years that followed, Siminoff continued to study the attributes of acoustic string instruments with a view toward understanding the contribution of each part to the overall sound. Fueled by the work of the great luthiery masters – from Stradivari and Guanari of the 1500s to Lloyd Loar in the early 1920s – Siminoff constructed numerous prototypes of a wide array of bracing and aperture models to test the premise of structural tuning.

In 1978, while working as a consultant for Gibson Inc., Siminoff shared his method for tuning soundboards and tone bars by measuring the component's deflection under a given load rather than trying to read its resonant frequencies in a noisy production environment. This process, which Siminoff coined "deflection tuning," continues to find favor with instrument builders and manufacturing companies worldwide.

In 1979, Siminoff was asked to write an instruction manual for the C.G. Conn Company (today part of Peterson ElectroMusical) entitled *The Secrets of Tuning Fretted Instruments*. This book described the basics of "tap tuning" and paved the way for using strobe tuners to build good sounding fretted instruments.

As an inventor, Siminoff holds six U.S. and three foreign patents for musical instrument designs.

Siminoff has authored several hundred articles on instrument construction and repair, musical acoustics, and the history and craftsmanship of musical instruments. His research and writings on the life and work of both Orville Gibson and Lloyd Loar have made him a highly respected expert on these renowned artisans. (For more information on Orville Gibson, Gibson company history, and Lloyd Loar, please visit www.siminoff.net.)

Also by Roger H. Siminoff:

Constructing a Bluegrass Mandolin
Constructing a 5-String Banjo
Constructing a Solid Body Guitar
The Luthier's Handbook
How to Set Up the Best Sounding Banjo
The Ultimate Bluegrass Mandolin Construction Manual